Political Campaigns

Other Books of Related Interest:

Opposing Viewpoints Series

The Federal Budget

The U.S. Supreme Court

Voting Rights

White Collar Crime

Current Controversies Series

Capitalism

Domestic Wiretapping

Federal Elections

Homeland Security

At Issue Series

How Does Religion Influence Politics?

Should the Federal Government Bail Out Private Industry?

"Congress shall make no law . . . abridging the freedom of speech, or of the press."

First Amendment to the U.S. Constitution

The basic foundation of our democracy is the First Amendment guarantee of freedom of expression. The Opposing Viewpoints Series is dedicated to the concept of this basic freedom and the idea that it is more important to practice it than to enshrine it.

Political Campaigns

Louise I. Gerdes, Book Editor

GREENHAVEN PRESS
A part of Gale, Cengage Learning

Detroit • New York • San Francisco • New Haven, Conn • Waterville, Maine • London

Christine Nasso, *Publisher*
Elizabeth Des Chenes, *Managing Editor*

For more information, contact:
Greenhaven Press
27500 Drake Rd.
Farmington Hills, MI 48331-3535
Or you can visit our Internet site at gale.cengage.com

Articles in Greenhaven Press anthologies are often edited for length to meet page requirements. In addition, original titles of these works are changed to clearly present the main thesis and to explicitly indicate the author's opinion. Every effort is made to ensure that Greenhaven Press accurately reflects the original intent of the authors. Every effort has been made to trace the owners of copyrighted material.

LIBRARY OF CONGRESS CATALOGING-IN-PUBLICATION DATA

Political campaigns / Louise I. Gerdes, book editor.
p. cm. -- (Opposing viewpoints)
Includes bibliographical references and index.
ISBN 978-0-7377-4540-5 (hardcover) -- ISBN 978-0-7377-4541-2 (softcover)
1. Political campaigns--United States. 2. Campaign funds--United States. 3. United States--Politics and government. I. Gerdes, Louise I., 1953-
JK2281.P65 2010
324.70973--dc22

2009036044

Printed in the United States of America
1 2 3 4 5 6 7 14 13 12 11 10

Contents

Chapter 2: What Strategies Promote Fair Political Campaigns?

Chapter 3: How Should Redistricting Be Managed?

Chapter 4: What Recent Developments Have Most Influenced Political Campaigns?

Why Consider Opposing Viewpoints?

> *"The only way in which a human being can make some approach to knowing the whole of a subject is by hearing what can be said about it by persons of every variety of opinion and studying all modes in which it can be looked at by every character of mind. No wise man ever acquired his wisdom in any mode but this."*
>
> *John Stuart Mill*

In our media-intensive culture it is not difficult to find differing opinions. Thousands of newspapers and magazines and dozens of radio and television talk shows resound with differing points of view. The difficulty lies in deciding which opinion to agree with and which "experts" seem the most credible. The more inundated we become with differing opinions and claims, the more essential it is to hone critical reading and thinking skills to evaluate these ideas. Opposing Viewpoints books address this problem directly by presenting stimulating debates that can be used to enhance and teach these skills. The varied opinions contained in each book examine many different aspects of a single issue. While examining these conveniently edited opposing views, readers can develop critical thinking skills such as the ability to compare and contrast authors' credibility, facts, argumentation styles, use of persuasive techniques, and other stylistic tools. In short, the Opposing Viewpoints Series is an ideal way to attain the higher-level thinking and reading skills so essential in a culture of diverse and contradictory opinions.

In addition to providing a tool for critical thinking, Opposing Viewpoints books challenge readers to question their own strongly held opinions and assumptions. Most people form their opinions on the basis of upbringing, peer pressure, and personal, cultural, or professional bias. By reading carefully balanced opposing views, readers must directly confront new ideas as well as the opinions of those with whom they disagree. This is not to simplistically argue that everyone who reads opposing views will—or should—change his or her opinion. Instead, the series enhances readers' understanding of their own views by encouraging confrontation with opposing ideas. Careful examination of others' views can lead to the readers' understanding of the logical inconsistencies in their own opinions, perspective on why they hold an opinion, and the consideration of the possibility that their opinion requires further evaluation.

Evaluating Other Opinions

To ensure that this type of examination occurs, Opposing Viewpoints books present all types of opinions. Prominent spokespeople on different sides of each issue as well as well-known professionals from many disciplines challenge the reader. An additional goal of the series is to provide a forum for other, less known, or even unpopular viewpoints. The opinion of an ordinary person who has had to make the decision to cut off life support from a terminally ill relative, for example, may be just as valuable and provide just as much insight as a medical ethicist's professional opinion. The editors have two additional purposes in including these less known views. One, the editors encourage readers to respect others' opinions—even when not enhanced by professional credibility. It is only by reading or listening to and objectively evaluating others' ideas that one can determine whether they are worthy of consideration. Two, the inclusion of such viewpoints encourages the important critical thinking skill of objectively evaluating an author's credentials and bias. This evaluation will illuminate an author's reasons for taking a particular stance on an issue and will aid in readers' evaluation of the author's ideas.

It is our hope that these books will give readers a deeper understanding of the issues debated and an appreciation of the complexity of even seemingly simple issues when good and honest people disagree. This awareness is particularly important in a democratic society such as ours in which people enter into public debate to determine the common good. Those with whom one disagrees should not be regarded as enemies but rather as people whose views deserve careful examination and may shed light on one's own.

Thomas Jefferson once said that "difference of opinion leads to inquiry, and inquiry to truth." Jefferson, a broadly educated man, argued that "if a nation expects to be ignorant and free . . . it expects what never was and never will be." As individuals and as a nation, it is imperative that we consider the opinions of others and examine them with skill and discernment. The Opposing Viewpoints Series is intended to help readers achieve this goal.

David L. Bender and Bruno Leone,
Founders

Introduction

> *"The Bipartisan Campaign Reform Act (BCRA) . . . accomplished precisely what it set out to do. The law broke the corrupting nexus between federal officeholders . . . and donors seeking to influence them."*
>
> *—Fred Wertheimer, President, Democracy 21*
>
> *"BCRA has achieved none of its goals. Instead, it created a muddy campaign finance environment that favors the political establishment."*
>
> *—Sean Parnell, President, Center for Competitive Politics*

Political corruption has troubled U.S. leaders since the nation's inception. Indeed, in *Federalist No. 10*, one of several essays advocating the ratification of the U.S. Constitution, James Madison warned that those elected to political office "by intrigue, by corruption, or by other means" might "betray the interests of the people." In the years since Madison wrote these words, Congress has tried to curb campaign abuses. In 1907, for example, Congress passed the Tillman Act, which prohibited corporations and national banks from contributing to candidates for federal office. The Publicity Act of 1910 required campaign finance disclosure, and in 1911 Congress amended the Publicity Act to place limits on campaign spending.

The greatest driving force behind political campaign reform over the years has been public scandal over political corruption. In 1925, for example, Congress passed the Corrupt

Practices Act in response to the 1924 Teapot Dome Scandal. Wealthy oilmen had bribed U.S. Secretary of the Interior Albert B. Fall to turn over control of rich oil fields on public land to the oil companies. In hopes of stemming such abuses, the act required political committees and congressional candidates to file contribution reports. Many thought, however, that the act was a failure due to numerous loopholes. It was not until 1971 that concern about the rising influence of money in politics led Congress to pass the more comprehensive Federal Election Campaign Act (FECA). FECA not only strengthened spending disclosure rules, but also placed limits on how much candidates could contribute to their own campaigns and what they could spend on television advertising. Following the Watergate scandal, which exposed abuses during the reelection campaign of incumbent president Richard M. Nixon, Congress further toughened FECA in 1974, adding even stricter limits and stronger disclosure requirements. It also established the Federal Election Commission (FEC) to administer and enforce FECA.

Opponents of the 1974 revisions challenged the constitutionality of the law. The resulting U.S. Supreme Court decision *Buckley v. Valeo* (1976) outlined two conflicting principles that have since framed the debate over campaign finance. One principle is that campaign "contribution" limits reduce corruption. The other, often conflicting, principle is that putting caps on "expenditures" restricts free speech. The Court argued that limiting campaign contributions outweighed First Amendment concerns because these limits helped prevent corruption and did not directly limit political discussion. The Court did, however, reverse limits on what candidates could spend on their own campaigns or what independent organizations could spend in support of candidates. These limits, the Court maintained, are a violation of the First Amendment protection of political speech. These conflicting principles have divided those in the debate over the most recent political campaign legislation—the Bipartisan Campaign Reform Act (BCRA) of 2002—into two main camps. On the one hand are those who believe the BCRA has succeeded in reducing corruption, and on the other hand are those who see the law as a restriction of political speech.

Those who see the BCRA as a success believe that the goal of the law was to reduce corruption. "The purpose was to break the corrupting link between federal officeholders who were raising unlimited six- and seven-figure contributions, and the donors who were providing these huge contributions to federal officeholders whom they were seeking to influence. It has done that," claims Fred Wertheimer, president of Democracy 21, a campaign finance reform advocacy group. BCRA critics counter that the act has not stemmed the flood of money into political campaigns. They cite the growth of independent, nonprofit organizations known as 527 committees that have spent hundreds of millions of dollars to influence elections. Indeed, argues political science professor David Primo, "If the goals were to reduce the amount of money in politics, [the BCRA has] been a colossal failure. . . . It hasn't changed the fact that donors with lots of money can use other groups" to influence the outcome of elections. Those who support the BCRA answer that the goal of the act was to reduce corruption, not money. "BCRA was never intended to limit 527 committees, whose rise was a predictable and inevitable result of BCRA's ban on large 'soft money' [indirect money contributed to organizations and committees] donations to political parties," reasons Loyola Law School professor Richard Hasen. "Both the potential for corruption and its actual appearance have lessened under this law," he concludes.

Critics who oppose campaign finance reform, claiming that it restricts First Amendment protected political speech, see the BCRA as a failure. "Instead of battling corruption, . . . BCRA simply added another layer of complex speech regulations that are only accessible to a limited class of citizens—the political elite," argues Sean Parnell, president of the Center for Competitive Politics. In fact, shortly after the act was passed, groups as diverse as the National Rifle Association (NRA) and the American Civil Liberties Union (ACLU) sought to have the act declared unconstitutional. Although the Supreme Court upheld the BCRA, dissenting justices revealed their concerns about BCRA provisions that might restrict political speech. Indeed, in a case involving ads run by the advocacy group Wisconsin Right to Life, a majority of the U.S. Supreme Court, led by Chief Justice John Roberts, undercut a BCRA provision that prohibits corporate funds from being used for certain political advertisements in the sixty-day period prior to an election. Wisconsin Right to Life ran ads shortly before an election asking people to contact two specific U.S. senators and tell these senators to support judicial nominees who supported their pro-life cause. The Court held that these were "issue" ads, not the "express advocacy" prohibited by the BCRA. Because the ads did not explicitly ask people to vote for or against a specific candidate, they should not be prohibited by the act. Restricting issue ads, BCRA opponents agree, restricts political dissent. James Bopp Jr., lead counsel for Wisconsin Right to Life, suggests, "The American Revolution was fought, and the First Amendment enacted, precisely to protect the people's right to criticize the government."

Supporters of the act believe that the Court erred in its *Federal Election Commission v. Wisconsin Right to Life* (2007) decision. According to Bob Edgar of the liberal advocacy group Common Cause, the Court has "gone a mile and a half too far in believing that money equals speech." In his view, such an interpretation means that those with money have a greater right to political speech than those who do not. "I don't think our Founding Fathers and Mothers ever intended money to equal speech." The current Supreme Court, these analysts assert, is likely to continue to support challenges to BCRA. "Obviously, the [campaign] reform side is going to do everything to fight" for continued reform, claims Meredith McGehee of The Campaign Legal Center. She maintains, "We're going to be in an uphill battle because this court is this court."

The campaign finance reform battle is clearly far from over. These two camps—those who believe campaign finance reform reduces corruption and those who contend it restricts political speech—continue to debate the effectiveness of the BCRA. In the following chapters, the authors in *Opposing Viewpoints: Political Campaigns* debate these and other issues surrounding political campaigns and the strategies that the authors believe will best promote fair elections: "What Is the Status of Campaign Finance Reform?" "What Strategies Promote Fair Political Campaigns?" "How Should Redistricting Be Managed?" and "What Recent Developments Have Most Influenced Political Campaigns?" Americans have long been concerned about political corruption. How best to promote fair, competitive campaigns and protect the political speech that the U.S. Constitution so vigorously defends is, therefore, quite contentious. Whether the two political campaign reform camps can in the future agree on how best to achieve these goals remains to be seen.

What Is the Status of Campaign Finance Reform?

Chapter Preface

One of several controversies in the campaign finance reform debate is whether the Federal Election Commission (FEC), the agency created to administer and enforce campaign finance laws, should be reformed. Created in the mid-1970s, the FEC is a body of six commissioners appointed by the president and confirmed by the Senate. Three commissioners are selected from each political party so that neither party will take politically motivated action against the other. As of June 2009, however, the FEC remains hopelessly deadlocked on the campaign finance issues before it. As a result, *The Wall Street Journal* has dubbed the FEC "The Little Agency That Wouldn't: wouldn't launch investigations, wouldn't bring cases, wouldn't even accept settlements that the staff had already negotiated." For many analysts, the fault lies with campaign finance reform itself. They favor the deregulation of campaign finance, which would make the FEC an administrative body. Others argue that the FEC simply has no teeth, no authority to enforce regulations. These observers suggest that the FEC would be more effective as a law enforcement body.

Those who oppose campaign finance reform overall contend that the FEC should be stripped of its regulatory power. Conservative columnist George Will maintains, "What if we [now] had deregulated politics—including the sort of presidential campaigns that produced 33 presidents (including some pretty good ones) . . . before the Federal Election Commission was created?" FEC opponents argue that there is no evidence that more regulation will reduce corruption or improve the campaign finance process currently in place. The FEC, they assert, should be limited to supervising campaign finance reporting and disclosure requirements. According to political science professor David Primo, "I've yet to see evidence that the political process or people's perceptions of government would somehow be fundamentally different in a negative way if we completely deregulated oversight of campaigns and just had disclosure requirements in place." Will agrees. "Government regulation of politics, as of most things, is perverse."

Those who support campaign finance reform believe that the FEC is deadlocked because it lacks enforcement ability. According to Fred Wertheimer of Democracy 21, the current FEC has no power to act on its own. In his view this makes the FEC a commission "framed in a message that its responsibility is to the regulated community, not the public." As created, these commentators claim, the FEC is the proverbial fox guarding the hen house. They suggest that Congress replace the FEC with a new, three-member agency—one that is politically independent and has greater enforcement power. In addition to administering campaign finance disclosure laws and the public-financing system, the new agency would have the power to make legal rulings on election-law disputes and impose penalties. Administrative law judges would work within this agency to help the three members rule impartially. "Rather than ultimately having commissioners from political backgrounds in charge of making conclusions about violations, you'd have impartial players," Wertheimer reasons.

Whether the FEC will be reformed is in large part up to Congress and the president. Commentators on both sides of the issue will continue to inflame this debate. The authors in the following chapter explore other controversies concerning campaign finance reform.

VIEWPOINT 1

"Under [the Bipartisan Campaign Reform Act] . . . there are multiple signs of revitalized parties, expanded grassroots activities, along with plenty of television and radio ads."

Campaign Finance Reform Is Working

Thomas E. Mann and Norman J. Ornstein

The Bipartisan Campaign Reform Act (BCRA) has reduced influence peddling and made campaigns more competitive, claim Thomas E. Mann and Norman J. Ornstein in the following viewpoint. BCRA does not decrease the amount of money in politics, but it reduces the threat that large donors are trading money for political influence, Mann and Ornstein maintain. Nor does the Act ban political speech, they argue. BCRA simply requires disclosure of the source of political ads. Mann and Ornstein are scholars at the Brookings Institution and the American Enterprise Institute, respectively.

Thomas E. Mann and Norman J. Ornstein, "Separating Myth from Reality in *McConnell v. FEC*," *Election Law Journal*, vol. 3, November 2, 2004, pp. 291–97.

As you read, consider the following questions:

1. What evidence do Thomas E. Mann and Norman J. Ornstein provide that the Bipartisan Campaign Reform Act (BCRA) has not starved the parties of resources?
2. How will reducing the demand for issue ads help political challengers, in the authors' opinion?
3. What evidence reveals that interest groups are still vital, in the authors' view?

Since BCRA [Bipartisan Campaign Reform Act] has taken effect, and especially since the Supreme Court's decision [in McConnell v. Federal Election Commission][1], critics, allied with political reporters who are generally cynical about any institutional reform and with the political consultants who were the conduits for and recipients of much of the soft money[2] in the pre-BCRA era, have pursued a series of themes perpetuating myths about the law and its impact.

Ironically, the two themes that have under-girded much of the message are to some considerable degree contradictory. On the one hand, this law is [in the words of William Goldcamp in *The Washington Times*] "in its own way, as great an attack on American liberty as the terror attacks of September 11, 2001," and does the greatest damage to liberty in America since the Alien and Sedition Acts. On the other hand, the law is so naïvely designed and filled with loopholes that it is toothless, filled with unintended consequences that undermine the law's intent. Whatever the themes, the attacks are built far more on myth than any reality about what is in the law or

1. In *McConnell v. the Federal Election Commission*, the U.S. Supreme Court upheld the constitutionality of most of the Bipartisan Campaign Reform Act of 2002 against claims that the legislation was an unconstitutional infringement on the petitioner's First Amendment rights.
2. Political money is often divided into two categories: "hard" and "soft." Hard money is contributed directly to a candidate or political party. Soft money is indirect money contributed to organizations and committees.

what we can detect thus far about its impact. The myths—and an initial assessment of the realities—include the following:

Myths and Realities

Myth 1: *BCRA was designed by naïve reformers to reduce the amount of money in politics, especially from special interests, and it is doing no such thing.* Of course, the prime proponent of this view is Senator Mitch McConnell. In his response to the Court's eponymous decision, Senator McConnell said, "This law will not remove one dime from politics." *The Washington Times*, in an editorial, said the reforms "are based on a utopian dream that some system can be concocted to make money meaningless in politics."

Reality: The objective of the new law was not to reduce the amount of money in campaigns, which are of necessity expensive and growing more so, but to break up the nexus among large donors, political parties, and elected officials. What reform did do is to sharply raise hard money limits on donations to candidates and parties even as most soft money (with its unlimited donation base) was eliminated. Reformers doubled hard money limits for individual donations to candidates, sharply raised the annual overall limits on what individuals could give, and created a separate large hard money limit for donations to national party committees—$100,000 a cycle for a couple. The shakedown scheme and access peddling that parties and officeholders were using with large donors who had no limits on what they could give appears to have largely disappeared. While the impact on the ground is real and pronounced, it has not been perfect; Rep. Tom DeLay, in particular, has made a move to use a charitable pretext to trade money for access, which is now under vigorous challenge from reform advocates. But in general, money for parties and candidates is coming in a very healthy flow, in a way that has sharply cut the routes of real and perceived corruption.

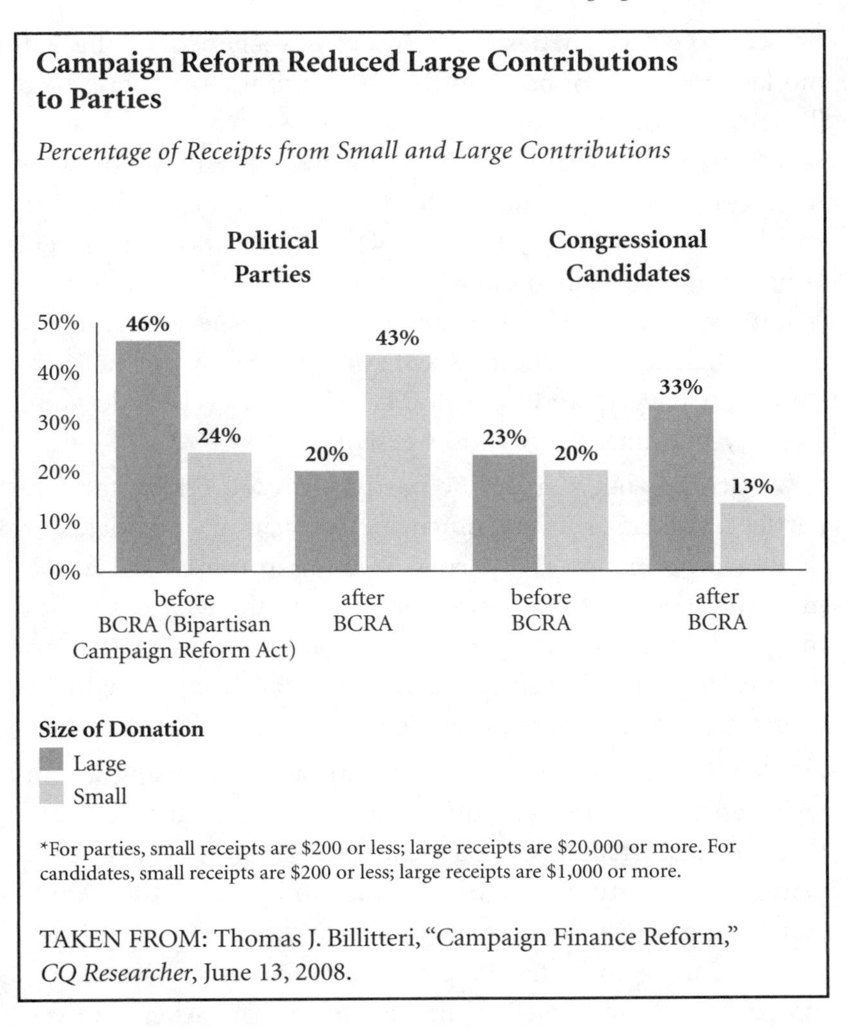

TAKEN FROM: Thomas J. Billitteri, "Campaign Finance Reform," *CQ Researcher*, June 13, 2008.

Political Parties Are Not Wounded

Myth 2: *BCRA is simultaneously weakening political parties and strengthening interest groups.* Said Republican campaign finance lawyer Benjamin Ginsberg, "The parties are much weaker and the special interest groups are much stronger." Added Jim Jordan, a former Democratic Senatorial Campaign Committee head, "Independent groups are now much more powerful than the parties."

Reality: The parties were actually weakened in the soft money era by becoming funding conduits for otherwise large illegal contributions; by concentrating resources in a handful of competitive races while shirking investments to broaden their competitive position in others; and by neglecting their small donors in favor of huge soft money contributors. The large amount of soft money going to the parties was illusory; it largely went right out the door into "issue ads" for and against federal candidates, except for the healthy cut taken by campaign lawyers and consultants, with relatively little going to party-building or grassroots activities.

BCRA has not starved the parties of resources. In fact, the parties are adapting very much in the fashion anticipated by BCRA's proponents. The parties have raised more hard money in the first year of this presidential cycle than hard and soft money combined during the comparable period in the last. Both parties are focusing heavily on small donors, with the Democrats making an unprecedented effort in this regard.

Republicans [in 2004] have a natural fund-raising advantage—apart from BCRA—due to their core constituencies and their control of the White House and Congress. Their party committees continue to enjoy an advantage over the Democrats. But a deeper look at the numbers shows that Democrats are not only likely to have the resources they need to compete, but are doing quite well in the era of reform. After one year under BCRA, the DNC [Democratic National Committee], for the first time in its history, closed the year with a major surplus, with over $10 million cash in hand and no debt. The party raised over $12 million in the fourth quarter of 2003; in the fourth quarter of 1999, the last pre-presidential year and a year in which both hard and soft money existed at the national level, the party collected $5.5 million. The total hard money raised by the DNC in 2003, $42 million, is more than 50 percent higher than the hard dollars raised in the comparable year 1999, and nearly as much as the total, hard and soft, raised that year—one in which the Democrats controlled the White House!

Mobilizing Grassroots Donors

Moreover, the Democratic Party has created a sophisticated set of programs to expand its small donor base, and built a centralized voter-contact and fund-raising system (called "Demzilla") to expand the donor base among those able to give the maximum. In the process, the DNC increased its direct mail donors from 400,000 to more than 1 million, and raised almost $32 million in small donations, an 85 percent increase over the comparable year 1999. [DNC] Chairman Terry McAuliffe, the architect of this plan, noted, "The fundamental structure of our fund-raising apparatus has changed. The average direct mail donation is only $37."

The robust financial activities within the Democratic Party are not limited to the DNC. The major Democratic candidates for president have raised nearly as much hard money combined as President George [W.] Bush, the most active and prodigious political fund-raiser in history. And the pathbreaking fund-raising efforts of Howard Dean over the Internet, bringing tens of thousands of new small donors into the process, shows considerable promise of having long-term benefits for the Democratic Party. Dean has already used this base to provide fund-raising openings for competitive Democratic congressional candidates and is working cooperatively with Chairman McAuliffe.

On the surface, the Democrats' congressional campaign committees are being significantly out-raised by their Republican counterparts. But a deeper look shows a much more competitive scene; congressional Republicans rely much more heavily than their Democratic counterparts on direct mail fund-raising, which is extremely expensive. Take out the fund-raising costs and look at cash on hand, and the numbers are very different. Because the Internet is nearly costless as a fund-raising tool, it has the potential for Democrats to develop and exploit funding from a vast new base of donors.

In sum, both parties will be in a financial position to play on a larger field of House and Senate races and to increase their grassroots mobilization efforts. Indeed, 2004 is shaping up as an election in which a premium is put on voter identification and mobilization.

While independent groups, including the so-called "527s," are active and operating (as the name suggests and the law requires) independently of the parties, much of the effort on the part of liberal groups like America Coming Together and the Partnership for America's Families is also directed at voter mobilization and get-out-the-vote efforts, which is less a challenge to the parties or a mechanism that will undermine them than a complementary set of activities to engage more Americans politically. Moreover, a clearheaded look shows that the amount these groups actually have raised is far behind what the parties have accomplished. Finally, serious legal questions exist about the ability of these groups—specifically political committees whose avowed purpose is to influence federal elections—to accept "soft money" contributions.

As for corporations, anecdotal evidence suggests that much of their soft money appears destined to stay in corporate treasuries. Corporate officials we have talked to say that their soft money donations were often coerced or given as access insurance to counter their rivals. They show no signs of a burning desire to give the money to independent groups; most seem delighted to keep it in their corporate coffers. To be sure, many corporations are now turning their efforts to expanding their executives' involvement in political action committees—an expansion of individual participation in politics through a common interest, which we, along with most reformers, consider legitimate and in no way either an unintended consequence or pernicious effect of reform.

Incumbents Are Not Protected

Myth 3: *The law is an incumbent-protection act that will further damage challengers.* Said James Bopp Jr., general counsel at the James Madison Center for Free Speech, the law "is an orgy of incumbent protection."

Reality: In 1976 and 1978—the first two elections run under the post-*Buckley*[3] hard-money regime and the two just before party soft money was created by the Federal Election Commission—the reelection rate for House incumbents was 95.8 percent and 93.7 percent, respectively; for Senate incumbents, it was 64 percent and 60 percent. In 2000 and 2002, the most recent elections fought under the soft money system championed by reform critics, the reelection rate for House incumbents was 97.8 percent and 95.9 percent; for Senate incumbents, it was 79.6 percent and 88.9 percent. So much for the salutary role soft money and so-called "issue ads" run by parties and groups played in helping challengers! While BCRA was not explicitly designed to increase competition in congressional elections, several of its provisions may contribute modestly to that objective. Perhaps its most significant boost to challengers will be its doubling of hard-money individual contribution limits, which, according to the Campaign Finance Institute, will benefit challengers more than incumbents. In addition, with parties no longer able to concentrate resources in a handful of races with soft money–financed issue ads, it is likely that more challengers will receive party assistance. Moreover, it is clear that the explosion of soft money–financed television ads by parties and outside groups both crowded out candidates' messages and sharply increased their broadcast costs. For challengers, getting over the threshold of recognition that all incumbents have is crucial, and higher television costs and greater cacophony make that threshold

3. In *Buckley v. Valeo (1976)*, the U.S. Supreme Court upheld the constitutionality of the Federal Election Campaign Act of 1971, a federal law that set limits on campaign contributions, but ruled that spending money to influence elections is a form of constitutionally protected free speech, and thus struck down portions of the law.

painfully higher. Reducing ad demand by parties will help challengers by lowering costs and freeing up more of the most potent time slots for candidate ads close to the election.

No Threat to Speech

Myth 4: *Citizens and their surrogate groups will lose their ability to speak freely and critically about the government and their elected representatives close to an election*. Nat Hentoff, in a post-*McConnell* column, said that citizens who rely on groups like the National Rifle Association (NRA) or the ACLU as surrogates to amplify their views through "issue ads" would be stifled because "the new 'reform' law forbids such 'electioneering communications' on television or radio that refer to specific candidates for federal office within 30 days before a primary or 60 days before a general election."

Reality: Never mind that throughout its history before the passage of BCRA, the ACLU never had occasion to broadcast ads now caught in the net of electioneering communications. No speech is banned by the new law—not a single ad nor any word or combination of words would be or has been muzzled. The only new requirements relate to the disclosure and sources of funding for television and radio ads close to an election that feature federal candidates and that are targeted to the races in which these candidates are running. The Court accepted the voluminous research that showed the overwhelming majority of these ads were indeed aimed at electing or defeating candidates, and accepted the congressional provisions that treated the ads in a fashion parallel to campaign ads that are paid for with hard money. As a January 7, 2004 AP [Associated Press] story by Liz Sidoti noted, ad spots by independent groups "still fill the airwaves" in both Iowa and New Hampshire before their presidential caucuses and primary. Some of the ads do not mention specific candidates, while others are financed through hard money. Kathleen Hall Jamieson of the Annenberg Public Policy Center noted of this phenomenon, "It shows that hard money lives." As for the vitality of interest groups, consider the following comments by the National Rifle Association's Wayne LaPierre. Noting the NRA would shift some energy to avenues other than television advertising and would expand efforts to raise hard money through its political action committee, LaPierre said, "We're going to be heard, I promise that. We have new lines on the football field, but the game is still going to be played."

With a year's experience under BCRA to draw on, there is no appreciable evidence that the political landscape is pocked with the debris of shattered parties, shackled and muted groups and individuals, or any other deleterious developments in the campaign funding system or the election process. Instead, there are multiple signs of revitalized parties, expanded grassroots activities, along with plenty of television and radio ads. The ads, to be sure, seem to be qualitatively different, possibly because of a little-noticed provision of BCRA originated by Rep. David Price (D-NC) called "Stand By Your Ad." As candidates take more public responsibility for the ads they run, we might see fewer petty personal attacks. Only time and systematic research will tell.

Money has neither dried up nor overwhelmed the process; new hard money, especially from a substantially expanded base of small donors, is coming in at a very healthy rate. There are few signs of the open bazaar selling officeholders' access in return for campaign cash. This is not a brand new world of campaign finance and political activity, but something reminiscent of the political world of the late 1970s and 1980s. Contrary to the judgment of some critics and in keeping with the view of the majority on the Court, we believe this is a world that reflects modest adjustments in the campaign finance regime under *Buckley*, not a world in which the *Buckley* structure will become irrelevant or unrecognizable. It also reflects the mature and sober view of reformers that no campaign finance regime will go long without the need for further incremental adjustments.

"Supporters grasp that changes in [campaign finance] rules—changes enacted in the name of ethics—can enhance their influence and foster their political aims by silencing their political opponents."

Campaign Finance Reform Is Not Working

Bradley A. Smith

Campaign finance reforms are not working, particularly because they violate free speech by silencing political opponents, argues Bradley A. Smith in the following viewpoint. Campaign finance reformers claim that laws are necessary to prevent corruption and promote ethical political campaigns. Smith claims, however, that campaign finance regulations do not promote political competition. Indeed, he reasons, they protect incumbent politicians by silencing criticism of those in public office. Smith asserts that studies show that corporate contributions have little actual political influence. Smith, former chairman of the Federal Election Commission, is a law professor at Capital University in Columbus Ohio.

Bradley A. Smith, "John McCain's War on Political Speech," *Reason*, vol. 37, December 2005, p. 36.

As you read, consider the following questions:

1. According to Bradley A. Smith, what are some of the monetary limits of the Federal Election Campaign Act (FECA)?
2. What does the author think is odd about how policy makers approach restrictions on political contributions?
3. Why, in the author's view, does political giving seem to be "consumption" rather than "investment" spending?

Polls consistently show that campaign finance reform is an extremely low priority for most Americans. It's not an issue that Americans wake up thinking about, even while pondering politics. It may seem like an obscure regulatory system that has very little effect on our daily lives, or even our political lives. But it's an assault on the First Amendment and a transfer of power from citizens to incumbent politicians, one that doesn't address far more serious conflicts of interest, including those of politicians who bang the campaign finance drum the loudest. As I step down as chairman of the Federal Election Commission, I fear that the regulatory machinery set in motion by Sens. John McCain and Russ Feingold will be used to further grind down the free expression of individual citizens.

An Overview of the Law

Before I discuss this, here is a very limited overview of what we call the limits, prohibitions, and reporting requirements of the Federal Election Campaign Act, or FECA.

FECA's provisions create a very complex matrix that depends on who is giving to whom. But to oversimplify, individuals can give a candidate no more than $2,200 per election; a political action committee (or PAC), which is merely a group of people pooling their small contributions, can give up to $5,000 to a candidate per election; and an individual can give up to $5,000 to a PAC per year. There are other limits on how much you can give to political parties, and there are overall limits on how much a person can give in a two-year period, but to keep this simple I want to focus on contributions by people to candidates. The list of prohibitions also includes bans on direct contributions by corporations, labor organizations, federal contractors, or foreign nationals to candidates and committees. Additionally the law prohibits the conversion of campaign funds for personal use, and then there are a wide variety of reporting requirements, things that have to be reported to the federal government, including the name, address, and occupation of donors contributing over $200—creating a sort of federal database of citizen political activity.

Silencing Criticism

In the legislative record there is considerable evidence that many supporters of McCain-Feingold [also known as BCRA, Bipartisan Campaign Reform Act] specifically wanted the law to silence criticism of their own performance in office. The act includes a provision that prohibits most citizen groups, such as the National Rifle Association, the Sierra Club, and Planned Parenthood, from making any broadcast advertisements within 60 days of an election that even mention a candidate for federal office.

You can easily find quotes from across the political spectrum explaining why members of Congress find the speech of these citizen groups distasteful. But for brevity's sake, let's focus on Sen. McCain. These groups, he once said, "often run ads that the candidates themselves disapprove of." What a horrible thought: citizens running ads that candidates disapprove of.

Sen. McCain went on: "Further, these ads are almost always negative attack ads, and do little to further beneficial debate and healthy political dialogue." Now, when Sen. McCain called my colleague on the FEC, Ellen Weintraub, "corrupt" merely because she disagreed with him on the proper interpretation of the law, I don't think *that* necessarily promoted healthy political dialogue. But should he be banned from saying it? No.

In his brief to the Supreme Court, Sen. McCain said, "These ads are direct, blatant attacks on the candidates. We don't think that's right." Well, I'll bet they don't. But the question is why we, as citizens, should be banned from having groups to which we belong, to which we've contributed money, which represent us and our beliefs, run ads that criticize officeholders, simply because the ads are "negative" or expose things about candidates that the candidates would rather not have exposed.

The odd thing is that we approach restrictions on political contributions on the theory that elected officials will tend, both in actuality and appearance, to place their personal interests in retaining office ahead of the public good, and shape public policy in the interest of campaign donors, even when those policies are opposed by their constituents and perhaps even themselves. And yet, in order to combat this alleged problem, we turn around and suggest that these same elected politicians should be given great deference because surely they would not pass campaign finance rules in order to handcuff their challengers. *Of course* they would have only altruistic motives in passing this kind of law.

Do Contributions Get Results?

Do campaign finance rules improve government ethics? In theory, they exist to prevent influence peddling. There is another angle from which we might talk about political contributions, and that is to presume that the giving is not voluntary, but rather the result of extortion by officeholders. I think there is some anecdotal evidence to support this view, and that it is more credible than the notion that corporations are trying to buy influence. There have been statements by execu-

tives who felt they were being shaken down; some episodes in which executives or others interpreted ambiguous public statements or letters by politicians as veiled threats; and incidents in which a successful corporation without a history of political giving suddenly opened up its checkbook after being subjected to a seemingly senseless regulatory legal assault by the government—such as what happened to Microsoft a few years ago.

From an ethical standpoint I'm not sure it matters much whether one calls it "extortion" or "influence seeking." They are flip sides of the same coin, and they are based on the idea that contributions will buy results in Congress. But the empirical evidence simply does not support this thesis.

Literally dozens of studies have been conducted trying to isolate the effects of campaign contributions on legislative behavior. And the substantial majority of these found no statistically significant impact. A small minority of the studies have located some correlation but have also found that the effect is distorted by several other factors, including ideology, party position, and constituent desires.

It's hard to isolate and measure political influence, and promoters of broad restrictions on corporate political activity have criticized these studies for precisely that reason. Nevertheless these surveys represent the best information we have, and they show that there isn't really a measurable problem. Regulatory enthusiasts like to say, "Well, those for-profit corporations must be getting *something* for their investment," but corporations give roughly 100 times as much to charity without getting much more than some decent P.R. and a sense of well-being. And we know from studies that corporate executives often act in ways contrary or tertiary to maximizing profits—by, for instance, choosing relocation sites based simply on where they'd prefer to live.

Similarly, most political giving seems to be "consumption" rather than "investment" spending. Corporate executives make more personal and corporate contributions because they simply like making contributions, whether because it fits their ideology, because it makes them feel like big shots, because they get invited to rub shoulders with politicians, or because they enjoy doing what they see as their civic duty—being a "good corporate citizen."

Whatever the motivation, do these corporate contributions actually buy "undue" influence? Even before McCain-Feingold, only about half of the *Fortune* 100 made soft money contributions. That suggests right away that the idea that political giving is a bottom-line plus for firms is suspect; obviously, half the firms don't think so.

No Measurable Adverse Effect

But what of those who *do* make contributions? If a *Fortune* 100 company's profits are roughly $5 billion a year, and the company makes $500,000 in political contributions in a two-year election cycle (an amount few donors ever reach), and if the firm further receives a 100 percent return on those soft money contributions, the profit would amount to about 0.01 percent of the corporation's two-year profit. That's hardly enough to matter. But suppose even that they were getting a 1,000 percent return on investment—meaning about 0.1 percent of the company's profits over two years—or even something higher: Wouldn't that nefarious influence purchasing be reflected in their stock prices?

And here is where the work of three economists at the Massachusetts Institute of Technology, led by Stephen Ansolabehere, is relevant. Ansolabehere's group divided the *Fortune* 500 into three groups: 216 companies that did not make soft money contributions, 142 that were modest donors (giving up to $250,000), and 142 large donors who gave more than $250,000. From the latter group, they also looked at a super-donor list of 50 who gave $1 million or more.

The researchers studied stock prices in the wake of five events related to campaign finance reform: the passage of the McCain-Feingold bill in the House of Representatives; the passage of the bill in the Senate; the signing of the bill into law by the president; oral arguments in the Supreme Court (at which Chief Justice William Rehnquist, who previously supported such restrictions, indicated that he had changed his position, which many people thought would make the Court much more likely to strike down the law); and the announcement of the Supreme Court decision upholding the soft money ban.

Were political donors penalized by the capital markets after the soft money ban? No. All these events had no measurable adverse effect on the stock valuation of these companies. If anything, it was the opposite. When the Supreme Court announced its decision on December 10, 2003—the most definitive event upholding the soft money ban—non-donors' stock suffered more than the stock of moderate donors, moderate donors did not do as well as large donors, and large donors did not do as well as the subset of million-dollar donors. Similarly, on the day the Senate passed the bill, large donors did the best of all, followed by moderate donors, and then non-donors. Now, most of these findings did not rise to the level of statistical significance. But the few that did indicated that the ban on soft money actually helped companies that had been making soft money donations. In short, none of the evidence supported the thesis that corporations were buying beneficial results. . . .

Looking Ahead

So what's next? Right now the FEC is conducting a rulemaking that could regulate the Internet. Because the McCain-Feingold bill did not mention Internet regulation in its list of terms, we at the FEC passed a rule exempting online speech. So Reps. Christopher Shays (R-Conn.) and Marty Meehan (D-Mass.), the main House sponsors of McCain-Feingold, filed suit, joined by Sens. McCain and Feingold in an amicus brief. They argued that the Internet exemption was improper and got a federal district court judge to agree. This rulemaking is the result. [For up-to-date Federal Election Commission rulemaking see www.fec.gov/law/Law_rulemakings.shtml.]

What will come of it, I don't know, but I'll tell you this: Right now in First Amendment jurisprudence there is more protection for simulated child pornography, flag burning, tobacco advertising, or burning a cross in an African American residential neighborhood than there is for running an advertisement that merely mentions a congressman's name within 60 days of an election. And why?

We're told this is to prevent corruption and to promote ethics. Well, I would suggest that ethics and government are served by political *competition*, and that regulation of campaign finances in fact serves as protectionism for incumbent politicians. It diminishes the relative influence of individuals and political parties, thus increasing the relative influence of politicians, corporate lobbyists, the media, and large foundations. At the same time it strikes at the very heart of self-government, which depends upon the idea that individual citizens outside of Washington can engage in an open exchange of ideas and criticisms of today's powers that be.

But perhaps most important, campaign finance regulation is based on the notion that government must be empowered to act on and order the lives of citizens without influence or pushback from those very same citizens. The "reformers" believe that politics should be reserved for the folks inside the Beltway who can handle it. In short, McCain-Feingold supporters grasp that changes in the rules—changes enacted in the name of ethics—can enhance their influence and foster their political aims by silencing their political opponents. Until we recognize this, and recognize that the very purpose of the First Amendment was to prevent such changes in the rules, the war on political speech will continue.

VIEWPOINT 3

> *"For those hoping to destroy a candidate with a clever spot or a cheap shot, the key question is which campaign-finance loophole to use."*

Issue Ads Undermine Campaign Finance Reform

David Corn

By using loopholes to escape the monetary limits imposed by campaign finance laws, special interest groups can exert excessive influence on federal elections, maintains David Corn in the following viewpoint. In 2004 special interest groups escaped donation limits by establishing themselves as 527 tax-protected committees. These groups use unlimited donations to sponsor issue ads that attack opposing candidates, Corn asserts. Since the Federal Election Commission ruled that 527 committees are campaign groups in disguise, these groups are now looking for new loopholes, he claims. Corn is the Washington bureau chief at Mother Jones *and author of* The Lies of George W. Bush: Mastering the Politics of Deception.

David Corn, "Meet the New Mudslingers," *Mother Jones*, vol. 33, February 25, 2008, p. 15.

As you read, consider the following questions:

1. What does Fred Wertheimer claim is "the cost of doing business" for 527 groups, as reported by David Corn?
2. According to the author, how was the ban on "issue ads" modified by the Supreme Court in June 2007?
3. In the author's view, what effectively shut down the Federal Election Commission?

Forget Swift Boats,[1] this election year [2008] could become the battle of the armadas. Thanks to the success of misleading ads against John Kerry in 2004—as well as recent Supreme Court and Federal Election Commission actions—the current presidential contest promises to be more cacophonous and mud strewn than any in recent history, with a record number of down-and-dirty ads financed on the sly by big-money interests. Attacks bankrolled by "independent" groups—businesses, unions, and millionaires—and amplified by YouTube and reporters starved for news "will play a much greater role than ever before," predicts a top GOP strategist.

There's just one catch: Groups that make it their express aim to influence federal elections—campaign and party committees, for example—are limited to $5,000 contributions from individuals and can't take money from corporations or unions. But recruiting enough $5,000 donors to underwrite a multimillion-dollar ad buy is a chore. So for those hoping to destroy a candidate with a clever spot or a cheap shot, the key question is which campaign-finance loophole to use.

The 527 Committees

In 2004, the answer was 527 committees, named after the tax-code provision covering them. These groups can take unlim-

1. Swift Boat Veterans for Truth is a political group of former prisoners of war and veterans who operated Swift [patrol] boats during the Vietnam War. The group formed during the 2004 presidential campaign to oppose John Kerry's candidacy. They engaged in what many Kerry supporters described as a smear campaign, engendering the pejorative term "swift boating."

ited donations. Billionaire George Soros alone gave nearly $24 million to 527s that year, including America Coming Together and the Media Fund, which together netted about $140 million in support of John Kerry. On the GOP side, the Swift Boat Veterans for Truth and the Progress for America Voter Fund raised about $58 million, of which T. Boone Pickens pitched in $4.5 million.

The Federal Election Commission recently ruled that these four 527s had violated campaign-finance law—that they essentially were campaign groups in disguise and should have abided by the $5,000 limit. Yet for what amounted to nearly $200 million in illegal spending, the groups were fined, in total, only $2.4 million, three years after the fact—a punishment easy to dismiss as "the cost of doing business," in the words of Fred Wertheimer, president of the clean-campaign advocacy group Democracy 21.

Looking for Loopholes

Nevertheless, the FEC action has made some donors think twice about 527s, says Wertheimer—which is why political operatives are busy cooking up other stratagems. One involves funneling money to nonprofit advocacy groups like MoveOn and the NRA [National Rifle Association], known as 501(c)(4)s after another tax provision, for voter organization efforts and election-related ads. (Donations to these organizations, unlike those to educational and charitable nonprofits known as 501(c)(3)s, aren't tax deductible; many groups, such as the Sierra Club, have both a (c)(3) and a (c)(4) arm.) Under the 2002 McCain-Feingold act, these advocacy groups were banned from running "issue ads" directed at candidates within two months of a general election. But the Supreme Court modified that ban [in *Federal Election Commission v. Wisconsin Right to Life*] last June [2007]. Now a nonprofit could, say, run a spot just before election time noting that Candidate X once voted against building a wall on the Mexico border, warning that—cue the ominous music!—X is willing to let terrorists sneak into the United States, and exhorting viewers to call X to register their outrage. So long as the ad hasn't (officially) been coordinated with X's opponent and doesn't outright say "vote against X," it's fine. And here's the best part: There are no limitations on the size of a contribution to a (c)(4), nor do its donors have to be disclosed. Moreover, due to that same Supreme Court decision, unions and corporations can now directly finance their own issue ads, expanding the number of players who can slam—or slime—the candidates in 2008.

Wertheimer identifies a few outfits likely to emerge as major independent spenders this year. On the GOP side, a likely big player is Freedom's Watch, a (c)(4) founded last summer [2007]. In 2007 the group—whose top donor has been casino mogul Sheldon Adelson—spent at least $15 million to support the surge in Iraq, and according to spokesman Jake Suski, it plans to expand its operations in 2008. In the Democratic camp, strategists including Clinton White House chief of staff John Podesta and Service Employees International Union (SEIU) official Anna Burger have launched a 527 named the Fund for America to raise money and distribute it to (c)(4)s doing voter organization in 10 to 12 key states; a parallel entity headed by Tom Matzzie, the former head of MoveOn's Washington office, will produce issue ads aimed at undercutting the Republican nominee. The Fund for America is hoping to raise at least $100 million.

Testing the Legal Waters

The legality of this circuitous strategy, admits one Fund for America official, is not fully tested: "We've built into the budget a little money in the expectation that we're unintentionally going to go beyond the boundaries of the law. We know we'll get challenged and will have people watching us every step of the way." The good news for the independent spenders is that a congressional tussle over the appointment of commissioners

"527" Committee Contributions, 2008 Elections

Contributor	Total
Service Employees International Union	$34,534,324
Pharmaceutical Product Development Inc.	$ 5,469,390
Soros Fund Management	$ 5,250,000
Las Vegas Sands	$ 5,010,000
Shangri-La Entertainment	$ 4,850,000
Fund for America	$ 4,600,000
Institute for Student Achievement	$ 3,787,000
Friends Of America Votes	$ 3,531,425
United Brotherhood Of Carpenters	$ 2,786,690
National Assn. of Realtors	$ 2,584,447

TAKEN FROM: Center for Responsive Politics, 2009.

left the FEC with four of its six seats vacant at the start of the year [2008], effectively shutting it down. "If you believe there's no sheriff in town," Wertheimer says ruefully, "anything goes."

Sure enough, the primary season has already seen some sneaky independent action. Prior to January's [2008] Iowa caucuses, a (c)(4) called Common Sense Issues set up the Web site TrustHuckabee.com to recruit pro-Huckabee precinct captains—a blatant and probably prohibited scheme to create a parallel campaign infrastructure. ("They are looking at a lot of litigation," says a former FEC official who asked not to be identified. "This is way beyond anything anybody should try.") And a 527 named Alliance for a New America, financed in part by SEIU affiliates, ran issue ads in Iowa hailing John Edwards's anti-lobbyist proposals. The Alliance received $495,000 from Rachel "Bunny" Mellon, the 97-year-old daughter-in-law of industrialist Andrew Mellon. A lawyer holding power of attorney for Mellon is an Edwards supporter, and he refused to explain how the generous contribution had come about.

Clearly, political operators weren't very fearful of the FEC or IRS. The recent rule changes, though, could make Swift-Boat-style character assassination tougher this year. If a 527 or (c)(4) group funded by unlimited contributions produces ads attacking a candidate's past or fitness for office, it will be difficult for the group to claim them as issue ads. "I suppose a group can say, 'We'll file as a 527 not for the purpose of influencing the election, but to educate the public on the quality of the candidates,'" says Jan Baran, a veteran Republican campaign-finance lawyer. "But that would be skating on thin ice."

The Do-It-Yourself Option

Which leaves the DIY [do-it-yourself] option: There are no restrictions on how much an *individual* can spend to influence an election, as long as she or he doesn't coordinate efforts with a candidate or party. Though most big-money people prefer a degree or two of separation from bare-knuckle politics, this year's [2008] high stakes could nudge some in that direction. "There is the possibility a billionaire will spend $100 million on the presidential campaign 'just because I feel like it,'" says Democratic consultant Guy Molyneux. "There's the potential for a huge ratcheting up. And we will see some pretty tough stuff." After all, the lesson of 2004 was that it only takes one good ad campaign to undo a candidate.

"We're looking at an enormous shift in control from parties and candidates to outside groups," says the former FEC official. "For a candidate, this can mean a loss of control of your message. And this also covers congressional candidates. Imagine if three weeks before the election, someone dumps $600,000 into your House race and you have no idea who it is." Candidates, he adds, "should be scared. Very scared." Maybe voters, too.

VIEWPOINT 4

"[Regulating 527s] would be yet another step in the wrong direction for political speech."

Laws Regulating Issue Ads Violate Free Speech

Byron York

Fears that issue ads sponsored by special interest groups exert too much political influence are exaggerated, claims Byron York in the following viewpoint. Placing contribution limits on 527s, named for the tax code that covers them, is an overreaction and unnecessarily restricts political speech, he reasons. The better solution to balance the influence of 527s would be to increase individual campaign contribution limits, York maintains. Placing limits on 527 speech to prevent negative political speech against one candidate threatens freedom of speech for all, he argues. York is the White House correspondent for the National Review *and is author of* The Vast Left Wing Conspiracy.

As you read, consider the following questions:

1. What was the bad news Cleta Mitchell reported to the GOP, according to Byron York?

Byron York, "To Stifle or to Compete: That Is the Question of 527s," *National Review*, vol. 58, April 10, 2006, p. 16.

2. In the author's opinion, why will Republicans most likely vote for limits on 527s?
3. Why, in the author's view, are the fears over 527 spending exaggerated?

In June 2005, after the last financial-disclosure reports from the 2004 election had been filed and the final totals calculated, a group of Republican insiders gathered in a conference room at the National Republican Senatorial Committee's headquarters in Washington, D.C. The pollsters, politicians, lawyers, and lobbyists had been asked to come by Pennsylvania Republican senator Rick Santorum, who wanted them to hear how the GOP, while winning the presidency, the House, and the Senate, had nevertheless lost—big time: the 2004 fundraising contest for contributions to "527" organizations, those anything-goes groups that allowed financier George Soros to spend more than $24 million of his own money in the drive to defeat George W. Bush.

Good and Bad News

The group listened as Cleta Mitchell, a lawyer and campaign-finance expert, presented her study of 2004 financing. Mitchell began by showing how well the Republican party had performed in raising money the old-fashioned way: in so-called hard money contributions to party committees. In 2004, the three big Republican committees—the Republican National Committee, the National Republican Senatorial Committee, and the National Republican Congressional Committee—outraised the comparable Democratic committees by a huge amount: Republicans brought in $898 million, Democrats $679 million.

That was the good news. The bad news came when Mitchell described the contributions to groups outside the parties, especially the 527s. Of the ten biggest 527s in 2004, Mitchell explained, seven were pro-Democrat. Of the top twenty, she said, 15 were pro-Democrat. Those 15 pro-Democrat groups raised $359,338,378. The five pro-GOP groups raised $85,363,370. That disparity alone more than erased the GOP's lead in hard money fund-raising.

Mitchell explained that the Democratic lead did not come from any massive grassroots enthusiasm for the party; rather, individual Democrats like Soros—along with colleagues such as insurance magnate Peter Lewis and Hollywood mogul Stephen Bing—were simply more willing to put up large amounts than were individual Republicans. Of the top ten individual donors to 527s, six were Democrats, who gave a total of $82,576,110. The four Republicans in the top ten gave $22,685,199—and many of them gave only after becoming alarmed at the astonishing sums Democrats were giving.

Leveling the Field

In 2004, of course, Republicans had the formidable advantage of an incumbent in the White House. But in the future, Mitchell said, outside spending might well determine elections. "I said we're all playing the same game, but it's like baseball," Mitchell recalls. "Democrats play the political game under American League rules. Their 'designated hitter' is the vast web of outside groups. Republicans play the political game under National League rules, within the party and the candidate campaigns." There were two possibilities to level the field: Republicans could try to stop the 527s—to impose McCain-Feingold-style contribution limits on them—or they could leave 527s alone, get in the game, work hard, and catch up. Today, nine months later, the GOP is close to making its decision.

Advocates of the first course are being led by—no surprise—Sen. John McCain. He blames the Federal Election Commission for failing to rein in 527s in the last presidential race, and in early March he unveiled a formal proposal that would limit contributions to 527s to $25,000 per person per year. That means Soros's $24 million would be cut to $50,000 in the next two-year cycle. McCain's Senate proposal is supported by a similar measure in the House sponsored by Connecticut Republican Christopher Shays.

Restoring Influence

But it is in the House that another GOP plan has emerged, one cosponsored by the solid conservative Indiana Republican Mike Pence and the equally solid liberal Maryland Democrat Albert Wynn. Pence and Wynn would impose some new restrictions on 527s, mostly along the lines of requiring them to report contributions quickly and openly. But they would not impose any limits on contributions. And they would go a step farther: In a bid to restore influence to the traditional parties, they would repeal the limits on the total amount of money any donor can give in a two-year political cycle. Current law allows individuals to give $2,100 to a candidate in any given year, or $4,200 per cycle. It also caps individual contributions to a party committee at $26,700 per year. Those restrictions are well known. What is less well known is that the law also limits the total amount of all contributions any one person may give. That limit is indexed for inflation, and right now stands at $101,400—a combination of $40,000 for federal candidates and $61,400 for party committees.

What Pence and Wynn would do is remove that aggregate limit without touching the individual limits. So, under their plan, if a donor this year wanted to give the maximum $2,100 to all 231 Republican members of the House and all 15 Republicans up for reelection in the Senate, he would be free to do so. If he wanted to give the maximum allowed to each of the party committees, he would be able to do that as well. No individual giving limit would be broken, but the person's aggregate contribution would be much higher than allowed in the past.

It's far short of a repeal of McCain-Feingold, but it's a small step in the direction of giving donors more freedom and the political parties more support. And Pence sees doing that, and leaving 527s untouched, as real progress: "To the extent that 527s have found an effective way to participate in the American political process with greater freedom than the major political parties and outside organizations, then, rather than restrain the 527s, we should give greater freedom to political parties and outside organizations."

Reacting in Fear

For Republicans, the choice might seem easy; Pence-Wynn is a clear move away from the steadily increasing regulation of political expression. Yet many in the GOP—actually, most in the GOP—are instead leaning in McCain's direction. And the reason is not any principled belief in campaign-finance reform, but rather the fear that Democrats will use 527s to beat the hell out of Republicans in 2006 and 2008. GOP House aides who follow the situation believe that most House Republicans would vote for limits on 527s. And a key Senate aide says that a very large number—perhaps all—of the Senate's Republicans would support limits, and do it for nakedly political reasons. "Republican members believe that 527s are a bad thing, gnawing away at the vitals of our majority, and that what McCain supports means their elimination," the aide says. "No doubt the bad guys will just find another section of the tax code to abuse for anonymous giving and deadly attacks against Republicans, but for now, since Republicans don't like them, and McCain is scared to death about what they could do against him come primary time in '08, there's a marriage of convenience underway."

It would be an understatement to say that Republicans who oppose regulation on principle find the current situation disheartening. "From a conservative standpoint, it's clearly wrong to jump on the regulatory bandwagon for what's perceived as short-term partisan gain," says Bradley A. Smith, the former FEC chairman, who has been one of McCain-Feingold's most forceful critics. Adds Cleta Mitchell: "The thing that is so discouraging is that my party, which opposed McCain-Feingold, has become the party that throws in with the guys who want to regulate everything. It just gives me a sick feeling in the pit of my stomach."

Practical Politics Versus Principles

Talking with Mike Pence, one gets the sense he agrees but has to be a bit more diplomatic toward his fellow lawmakers. "There are many of my colleagues who are experiencing withering daily assaults from the 527s," he says. "They have been brought to the place where practical politics and principle collide." And in many cases, practical politics is winning.

Of course, it's not as if there is much principle on the other side. These days, Democrats who long championed McCain-Feingold's restrictions are adamantly opposed to extending them to 527s. New York's Charles Schumer, once a strong reformer and now head of the Democrats' Senate election effort, has cooled on the idea of cracking down on 527s.

It is entirely possible that more regulation is on the way. But ultimately, all the fears over 527 spending might be exaggerated. When analysts of both parties look back at the groups' activities in 2004, they see two major examples: the giant, Soros-funded, pro-Democrat turnout group called America Coming Together, and the smaller anti-Kerry operation Swift Boat Veterans for Truth. Which was more effective? It's hard to deny that the Swift Boat Vets got perhaps the biggest bang for their buck in political-advertising history. Most of that bang came at the very beginning, when the group had a relatively small amount of money. "At the time we filmed our first commercial, our total expenditure was around $350,000," recalls John O'Neill, the group's most visible leader. That $350,000 included $100,000 each from supporters T. Boone

More Speech Is What Is Needed, Not Less

Studies indicate that campaign spending diminishes neither trust nor involvement by citizens in elections. Indeed, spending increases public knowledge of candidates among all groups in the population. "Higher campaign spending produces more knowledge about candidates," [writes John J. Coleman], whether measured by name identification, association of candidates with issues, or ideology; and setting a cap on spending would likely produce a less informed electorate. Unlimited spending does not confuse the public, and the benefits of campaign spending are broadly dispersed across advantaged and disadvantaged groups alike. That is, as incumbents are challenged by spending, both advantaged and disadvantaged groups gain in knowledge. And so-called negative advertising campaigns do not demobilize the public, as many have alleged.

Stephen Hoersting,
Cato Institute Briefing Papers,
no. 96, April 3, 2006.

Pickens and Bob Perry, the kind of donation that would be banned under McCain's proposal. The relatively meager $350,000 paid for everything—for organizing, for travel, for a Web site, for producing the initial commercial, and for buying its airtime. Later, when the message caught on, millions in small donations came pouring in. But the Swift Boat Vets were never more effective than when their first ad aired. In contrast, America Coming Together started with zillions of dollars, which it never learned how to spend efficiently and effectively. It poured mind-boggling amounts of money into Ohio, and lost.

Threats to Free Expression

So what is the lesson? That 527s should be strangled? Doing so not only would run against Republican belief in freedom of expression, but would make it harder to score targeted political points in coming campaigns. That's something Republicans might come to regret in 2008 if they find themselves in a race against a certain senator from New York who was once a First Lady enmeshed in numerous scandals. "There are huge numbers of voters in America who have no knowledge of Travelgate, cattle futures, the whole thing," says Bradley A. Smith. "Who's going to talk about that for Republicans? Are they counting on CBS to do it?"

These days, however, Republicans seem more than willing to shut down the 527s. In the end, it is impossible to say whether 527 regulation would hurt or benefit either Democrats or Republicans. But it is possible to say that it would be yet another step in the wrong direction for political speech. "We are on the road to serfdom in American politics with campaign-finance reform," says Mike Pence. "We are eventually going to end up on the doorstep of George Soros's house, telling him what he can and cannot say." And not just Soros: T. Boone Pickens and Bob Perry, too. Republicans and Democrats alike.

[Editor's note: Neither McCain's proposal (S1053; revised S271) nor the Pence-Wynn bill (HR1316) became law. In a series of deadlocked votes that took place in closed sessions during the fall of 2008, the Federal Election Commission's three Republican members voted to reverse previously established limits on 527 political organizations.]

Viewpoint 5

> *"Research . . . provides comfort that caps on [political] contributions will promote, rather than hinder, competition."*

Placing Caps on Campaign Contributions Promotes Competitive Elections

Deborah Goldberg

Caps on contributions to political campaigns promote electoral competition, argues Deborah Goldberg in the following viewpoint. Critics claim that contribution caps protect incumbents, but studies prove otherwise, indicating the access incumbents have to vast sums of political contributions, she states. One 2004 study, for example, showed that incumbents raised four times more than their challengers. The U.S. Supreme Court has acknowledged the role contribution limits have played in preventing corruption, she maintains. Goldberg directs the Democracy Program at the Brennan Center for Justice at New York University School of Law.

As you read, consider the following questions:

1. According to Deborah Goldberg, what did the U.S. Supreme Court find in *Nixon v. Shrink Missouri Government PAC?*
2. According to the author, why were two lower courts persuaded to uphold Vermont's limits?
3. In the author's view, what are incumbents more likely than challengers to attract when limits are raised?

Contribution limits have been a core element of campaign finance regulation for decades, and the Supreme Court has repeatedly upheld them in the face of constitutional challenge. But opponents of Vermont's limits are now asking the Court to reconsider, arguing that caps on contributions are an incumbent-protection device.

However, three new studies on campaign contribution limits—one published in *Public Choice*, a second forthcoming in *Political Research Quarterly*, and the third to be published by the Brookings Institution in *The Marketplace of Democracy*—offer empirical evidence to quell that familiar but flawed argument.

The argument has risen in *Randall v. Sorrell*, a challenge to Vermont's ceilings on campaign spending and contributions. Vermont enacted the mandatory expenditure caps in a conscious attempt to test *Buckley v. Valeo*, the 1976 precedent widely understood to foreclose such caps. When *Randall* reached the Supreme Court, everyone knew the spending limits would be controversial.

But observers were surprised to see the extent of the Court's skepticism about the contribution limits. After all, *Nixon v. Shrink Missouri Government PAC* had reaffirmed the constitutionality of contribution limits just six years earlier. Why should Vermont's limits prompt questions?

Vermont allows contributions of $400, $300 and $200 per election cycle to candidates for statewide offices, state Senate seats and state House seats, respectively. In *Nixon*, the Court found that Missouri's limit of $1,075 per election for statewide candidates was not "so radical in effect as to render political association ineffective . . . and render contributions pointless."

Although the Supreme Court has never considered contribution limits as low as Vermont's, the lower limits should not be surprising for a state that ranks 49th out of 50 in both population and gubernatorial campaign spending.

Applying the *Nixon* standard, federal courts have upheld contribution limits comparable to, or even lower than, those in Vermont. Caps of only $100 per election for legislative candidates in Montana have withstood constitutional challenge. The courts in that case considered the facts pertinent to Montana and determined that its contribution limits met the Supreme Court's test.

The facts about Vermont, including its small population and low costs of media advertising, persuaded two lower courts to uphold Vermont's limits as well.

The Supreme Court soon will decide whether to affirm those decisions in *Randall*.[1] The facts in the record overwhelmingly support the lower courts' conclusion that Vermont's contribution limits are constitutional. The evidence shows that all candidates—incumbents, challengers and candidates for open seats—can conduct effective advocacy under the limits.

Concerns about the ability of challengers to compete also are allayed by new research on contribution limits. In their *Public Choice* article, economists Thomas Stratmann and Francisco Aparicio-Castillo found that contribution limits appear

1. Later in 2006, the Supreme Court decided *Randall v. Sorrell*, holding that Vermont's cap on political contributions hindered free speech and was, therefore, unconstitutionally too low.

The Campaign Cash Arms Race

As even the multimillionaires of the Senate will confirm, the arms race for campaign cash occupies far too much of a candidate's time and attention. Worse, it leaves many citizens wondering what debts were incurred in gathering the war chest. This kind of public cynicism about the electoral process is debilitating for our democracy. The time has come to change this with reasonable upper limits on candidates' campaign spending.

Brenda Wright,
National Law Journal,
June 27, 2005.

to help challengers in state Assembly elections. Such regulations are associated with both an increase in the number of challengers and a decrease in incumbents' reelection margins.

Two forthcoming studies focusing on gubernatorial elections reached similar conclusions. According to Kihong Eom and Donald Gross, analyses of both the number of contributors and the dollar amount of contributions to gubernatorial candidates suggest no support for an increased bias in favor of incumbents resulting from the presence of contribution limits. David Primo, Jeffrey Milyo and Tim Groseclose conclude that limits on individual contributions to candidates have statistically and substantively significant effects on the winning margins in gubernatorial races, narrowing such margins.

These recent statistical analyses of the empirical data comport with common sense. We all know that one of the principal advantages of incumbency is access to financial contributions, especially in larger amounts. In the 2004 cycle, for example, incumbents outraised challengers more than 4-to-1.

Incumbents increased their edge in contributions of at least $1,000 from $67 million in 2002 (the last cycle before the limits were doubled) to $178 million in 2004.

True, a few challengers might have wealthy supporters who could bankroll their candidacies if not for contribution limits. But the risks of corruption from such an arrangement outweigh the burden on the rare challenger backed by a millionaire. And, as we have seen, incumbents are far more likely than challengers to attract big money when limits are raised.

The Supreme Court has long recognized the role of contribution limits in combating real and perceived corruption. The only circumstance that has given supportive justices pause in recent years is the possibility that such limits would exacerbate a preexisting incumbent advantage. The new research on that subject provides comfort that caps on contributions will promote, rather than hinder, competition. If the factual record and the numerical evidence, rather than rhetoric and ideology, persuade the Court, then Vermont's limits will be upheld.

VIEWPOINT 

> *"The 'Millionaires' Amendment' is nothing more than incumbency protection disguised as a good-faith effort to cleanse our political system."*

Laws That Cap Spending of Self-Funded Candidates Are Unconstitutional

Ilya Shapiro

The "Millionaires' Amendment," the section of the Bipartisan Campaign Reform Act (BCRA) that limits the amount of money wealthy candidates can spend on their own political campaigns, is an unconstitutional restriction on free speech, claims Ilya Shapiro in the following viewpoint. The reasoning behind the law is to prevent wealthy candidates from buying a seat in Congress, he asserts. The amendment, however, actually promotes corruption by forcing candidates to depend on outside contributions—thereby opening themselves to outside influences—Shapiro reasons. Moreover, he maintains, the law limits the political speech of self-funded candidates while increasing the political speech of their opponents. Shapiro is editor in chief of the Cato Supreme Court Review.

Ilya Shapiro, "Valeo's Revenge," *American Spectator*, May 7, 2008.

As you read, consider the following questions:

1. According to Ilya Shapiro, what happens once a self-funded candidate reaches the law's $350,000 limit?
2. Under what circumstances does $350,000 not go very far, in the author's view?
3. What impact does the amendment have on potential corruption in political opponents, in the author's view?

As Pennsylvania Democrats went to the polls last month [April 2008] in the last big primary before the party's nominating convention, the Supreme Court heard yet another challenge to campaign finance regulation. Whether Barack [Obama] or Hillary [Clinton] finally wins the Democratic nomination, and no matter who wins the White House in November, the outcome of [*Davis v. Federal Election Commission*] will color the Congress the new president has to work with.[1]

The Reasoning Behind the "Millionaires' Amendment"

The "Millionaires' Amendment" of the McCain-Feingold law [also known as the Bipartisan Campaign Reform Act] discourages congressional candidates from using their own funds to finance their campaigns. The supposed reason for this blatant restriction on free speech is to prevent people from "buying" a seat in Congress, but its actual effect is to protect officials who've already been elected and who plan to stay that way.

When a candidate decides to run for Congress, he has to file, under penalty of criminal law, a statement of how much he intends to spend out of his own pocket. But if the amount is over $350,000 (less than a quarter of the expected cost of a House race this year), then his opponent—typically the in-

1. On June 26, 2008, the U.S. Supreme Court ruled that the so-called "Millionaires' Amendment" to the Bipartisan Campaign Reform Act was unconstitutional, violating the First Amendment.

cumbent—is allowed not to comply with some of McCain-Feingold's anti-corruption "reforms."

For example, the incumbent enjoys a tripling of the $2,300 individual contribution limit, and a total exemption from the restrictions on coordinating expenditures with the national party.

Moreover, once the "statement of intent" to spend over $350,000 is filed—or once the limit is reached, if it is reached unexpectedly, which could itself give rise to criminal and civil liability—then that self-funded candidate has to disclose every expenditure of $10,000 or more to his opponent within 24 hours of spending that money.

This disclosure signals the self-funded candidate's tactics, enabling his opponent to infer and counteract television and radio advertising, leafleting, and the like.

Gaining Strategic Advantage

So not only does the opponent of a self-funded candidate (again, almost always the incumbent) enjoy relaxed campaign finance restrictions, he gains a strategic advantage over his hapless challenger!

And remember, $350,000—a figure set in 2002 and not indexed to inflation—simply does not go far in competitive races. Especially when you're running against an incumbent who has built up a war chest, which doesn't count for calculating the "gross receipts differential" at the heart of the convoluted formula used to determine the extent to which the opponent can use the relaxed contribution and coordination limits.

Not to mention the other inherent advantages of incumbency: greater name recognition, "franking" privileges to get your message out to constituents without mailing costs, the ability to gain publicity by securing earmarks and otherwise going about your "public service," and, of course, taxpayer-funded travel home.

The Supreme Court's Decision in *Davis v. FEC*

While BCRA [Bipartisan Campaign Reform Act] does not impose a cap on a candidate's expenditure of personal funds, it imposes an unprecedented penalty on any candidate who robustly exercises that First Amendment right, requiring him to choose between the right to engage in unfettered political speech and subjection to discriminatory fund-raising limitations. . . . The burden is not justified by any governmental interest in eliminating corruption or the perception of corruption. Nor can an interest in leveling electoral opportunities for candidates of different personal wealth justify §319(a)'s [part of the so-called Millionaires' Amendment] asymmetrical limits. The Court has never recognized this interest as a legitimate objective and doing so would have ominous implications for the voters' authority to evaluate the strengths of candidates competing for office.

Samuel Alito, majority opinion,
Davis v. Federal Election Commission,
U.S. Supreme Court, June 26, 2008.

So instead of "leveling the playing field" between candidates for office, the Millionaires' Amendment further tilts it the incumbents' way. That's the other unfortunate aspect of this mess: Not only is this tremendously complex regulation bad policy, it's also unconstitutional.

An Unconstitutional Restriction

First, the provision burdens the exercise of political campaign speech without serving any compelling governmental interest. By enhancing the political speech of a self-funded candidate's opponent—through the increased contribution limits and unlimited coordinated party expenditures—it creates a *de facto* expenditure limit, in essence restricting speech beyond the $350,000 threshold. The Supreme Court ruled in the famous 1976 case of *Buckley v. Valeo* that expenditure limits were unconstitutional.

Second, the Millionaires' Amendment does not prevent actual or apparent corruption because there is no threat of a quid pro quo from a candidate spending his own funds. The provision actually undermines the stated interest in combating corruption by preventing candidates from reducing their dependence on outside contributions—and increasing their opponents' purportedly corrupt contributions and coordinated expenditures.

Finally, the compelled disclosure requirements further penalize candidates for exercising their right to engage in political discourse by imposing significant personal liability on them. The disclosure requirements also infringe on a candidate's First Amendment right *not* to associate with campaign contributors. And they do so without serving any informational interest the public may have, because the underlying information is already disclosed to the FEC under other McCain-Feingold requirements.

In short, the "Millionaires' Amendment" is nothing more than incumbency protection disguised as a good-faith effort to cleanse our political system, much like most campaign finance "reform."

Viewpoint 7

> *"Make all campaign donations secret so that nobody—especially political candidates—knows where any citizen's money is going."*

Public Campaign Financing Should Be Anonymous

Farhad Manjoo

One solution to campaign finance corruption is to give all voting Americans money to donate anonymously to the candidate of their choice, maintains Farhad Manjoo in the following viewpoint. Giving people a say in where their donations will go gives the public a reason to support public financing, he reasons. Current campaign finance laws are ineffective and encourage candidates to seek out loopholes. Public money, he asserts, should always be greater than private spending so that ordinary people have more campaign finance power than the wealthy. Manjoo is a staff writer for Salon.com.

As you read, consider the following questions:

1. According to Farhad Manjoo, why does reforming the system not have to be a pipe dream?

Farhad Manjoo, "How to Fix Campaign Financing Forever for $50," Salon.com, February 5, 2007. This article first appeared in Salon.com at http://www.salon.com. An online version remains in the Salon archives. Reprinted with permission.

2. When does the author claim the secret donation booth should come into play?
3. Why does the author believe Congress will not introduce the Bruce Ackerman and Ian Ayres plan?

Today's campaign finance regulations are as effective as abstinence vows on prom night, and the leading proposals to fix the system do little more than impose some decorum on the bacchanalia. This week [early February 2007] Sen. Russell Feingold, just about the last politician in the nation who can still muster any fervor on the issue, offered a plan that would modestly tweak the current system, increasing some public funding here and eliminating some limits there. The plan's prospects look uncertain. His former co-conspirator in reform, John McCain, says he's not even familiar with Feingold's idea, perhaps because as a presidential candidate he now spends much of his time asking rich people for money. But even if Feingold's plan did become law, it would do nothing about the fundamental problem. Running for office takes an enormous amount of money, and even though "You" may be Person of the Year, drunk on the power of "your" blogs and "your" YouTube, politicians will always be able to get more money from "Them," the fat cats.

An Unorthodox Proposal

But reforming the system doesn't have to be a pipe dream. In fact, there's already a plan out there that would work. The proposal, which was outlined a couple of years ago by Bruce Ackerman and Ian Ayres, two professors at Yale Law School, is nonpartisan, constitutional and completely contrary to nearly every orthodoxy in the campaign finance reform movement. Think of it as the best campaign finance reform proposal you've never heard of.

The first part of the Ackerman-Ayres plan calls on the government to give every voter $50 to donate to candidates running for federal office. The second part will sound almost as crazy, until it sounds brilliant: Make all campaign donations secret, so that nobody—especially political candidates—knows where any citizen's money is going. Anonymous giving means no quid pro quo.

What's Wrong with Campaign Finance Laws?

To understand what's so truly inspired about this proposal, you first have to understand what's wrong with today's laws. The current regulations were put in place to counter the abuses uncovered during the Watergate investigation, things like the Committee to Re-elect the President's maintenance of secret slush funds for dirty tricks [unethical methods of gaining advantages over opponents]. They mainly limit how much money individuals can donate to candidates and how much candidates can spend to win office. In return for abiding by spending limits, politicians get public matching funds—that is, money from the government—to mount their campaigns.

This may seem like a sensible approach, but Ackerman and Ayres suggest that it is fundamentally flawed. Capping how much money people can give to candidates only invites ways to get around those limits. Getting around the limits has become a huge Washington business, employing battalions of lawyers and lobbyists. Limits simply don't limit much—every election sees more private donations to candidates, and more money spent on campaigns.

Conservatives often argue that there's nothing wrong with candidates collecting all this money so long as they fully disclose it. Newt Gingrich, for example, wants politicians to have to post to the Web receipt of all donations within 24 hours of cashing the check. But we are already drowning in disclosure—go to OpenSecrets.org to feast on a smorgasbord of candidates' funding sources—and it has hardly changed a thing. Public knowledge of politicians' funders perhaps deters the worst kind of influence peddling, outright bribery. But disclosure does nothing to stem more pervasive forms of favor trading. There is no better illustration of this than the current president, who won his office thanks to wheelbarrows of cash from business interests, notably the oil and gas industry, a sector few Americans hold in high regard. Public awareness of who backed George W. Bush has not mitigated his willingness to act in accordance with those backers' interests. As *Slate*'s [magazine] Timothy Noah recently observed, sometimes sunlight just isn't so great a disinfectant.

When you mention these difficulties to reformers, they often respond by suggesting the most radical change of all: complete public financing of elections. Under this plan, the government would pick up the entire tab for candidates' electioneering efforts. While that has obvious benefits—public money frees up candidates to focus on policies rather than fund-raising, and it leaves them beholden to no one—there is one huge drawback. The public is opposed. The current system of public matching funds is paid for by taxpayers who check off a box on their tax forms directing $3 to candidates. In the 1970s, more than a third of taxpayers checked off the box. Now, only 1 in 10 do, and the number is dropping. If the people aren't willing to direct $3 to candidates, how can we expect them to go for anything more?

A Reason to Support Public Financing

It's here that we come to what's great about the Ackerman-Ayres plan: It offers the public a reason to support public financing. Today, people have no say in how their $3 is spent. Under the new plan, anyone who registered to vote would receive $10 to donate to House candidates, $15 to Senate candidates and $25 to presidential candidates. They could make their pledges essentially any way they chose. They could fund long shots or front-runners, spend their wads in the primary or the general election, in their home state or across the nation. They could split their allotments among dozens of contenders or just choose one Senate candidate, one House candidate and one presidential candidate. They could not cheat and spend the money on dinner. The $50 would be issued as a kind of electronic voucher that would expire on Election Day, and Ackerman and Ayres suggest that people could register their donations using the Web, ATM machines or even their electronic food stamp cards.

About 120 million people voted for president in 2004. At $50 each, that would be $6 billion in public financing available for candidates, more than enough to fund big campaigns. As a comparison, all federal candidates—for the House, the Senate and the presidency—spent a combined $4 billion in 2004, most of it raised from private donors. Such sums would profoundly alter the political process. Today, Ackerman and Ayres point out, many Americans participate in politics only at the end of a long campaign, if they do at all. Fifty dollars isn't a fortune, but it's more than most voters give. By pooling the money, candidates would be forced to recognize issues of real importance and campaign in places they might otherwise deem pointless to visit. In search of donations, Republicans might even come to San Francisco.

The plan wouldn't prevent you from giving a politician more than your government-issued $50. You could still make additional private contributions. Indeed, the professors call for raising *significantly* the current contribution limit of $2,300 per donor per candidate. The new caps would be $5,000 for House candidates, $32,000 for Senate candidates and $100,000 for presidential contenders (with a cumulative cap of $100,000 to all candidates). But that's where Ayres and Ackerman's second innovation, the "secret donation booth," comes into play.

The Secret Donation Booth

Imagine that you are a politically connected Hollywood producer, and Hillary Clinton calls you up and asks you for

What Do Americans Think About Campaign Spending?

Has too much been spent on the presidential campaigns?

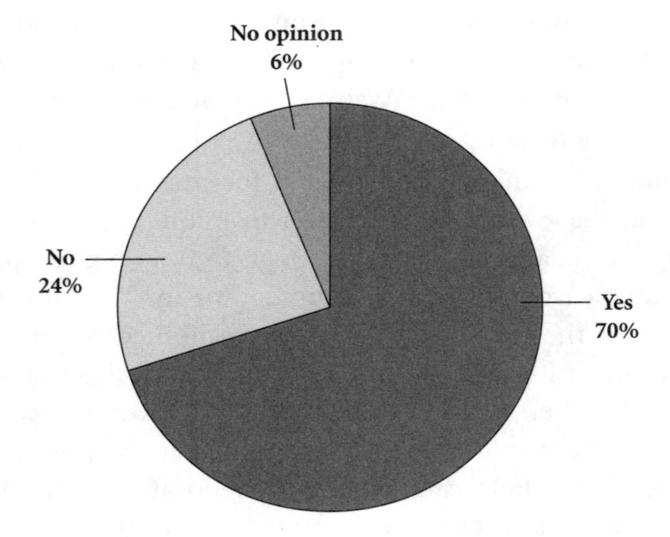

Should spending be limited or should candidates be able to spend whatever they can raise?

TAKEN FROM: Poll of 1,008 adults. Margin of error: ±3 percentage points. *USA TODAY*, October 29, 2008.

$50,000. What do you do? In truth, you'd rather give to Barack Obama, whom you consider more electable, but you don't want Clinton to know that. After all, what if she wins? Then you'll never see the inside of the Lincoln Bedroom. So you tell Clinton that you're definitely on her side. Fortunately, under the Ackerman-Ayres plan, you'll make your check out to the Federal Election Commission, not Clinton. The FEC will wait five days before adding your money to Clinton's account. In those five days, you could contact the FEC and redirect the money to Obama if you chose. And regardless of which candidate ultimately gets the money, its origin will be masked. The FEC will distribute the cash to the candidate's account anonymously, in pieces, over several days, using a secret algorithm to vary the pattern by which it deposits the money. So even though you promised the New York senator your support, she'll have no way of knowing whether you really went through with it. You could send your money to Obama and Clinton would have no way of knowing whose side you were actually on.

The professors compare their anonymous donation mechanism to an electoral innovation that we now think of as sacrosanct—the secret voting booth. Early American elections were conducted in the open, a situation that led to a rash of vote buying. But in the late 19th century, as states switched over to secret ballots, the practice of bribing people to vote a certain way dropped dramatically. Today only a foolish candidate would pay you to vote for him. You could take his money and swear on your mother's grave that you'll vote accordingly, but once in the privacy of the voting booth, you can do whatever you please.

The secret donation booth could have the same effect on today's main political transaction, wherein candidates, with a wink and a nudge, offer donors electoral favors. Certainly many wealthy people would still want to give candidates a lot of money, and certainly candidates would still promise great possibilities to their donors. But, theoretically, suspicion would sour the money parade, significantly reducing overall donations. Today's routine $2,000-per-plate benefits would become impossibly tense affairs. If they didn't like the veal, CEOs might go home and secretly cancel their checks, and the candidates would never know. Meanwhile, any politician would be foolish to risk losing public favor—which, remember, would be worth billions—by kowtowing to a big donor's unpopular ideas, because the politician could never truly know that the donor ever gave a dime.

You might argue that donors would find other ways to suggest to candidates that they're team players. Perhaps the nation's energy executives could visit Dick Cheney—privately, of course—and assure him that they're giving gobs of money. Because of constitutional restrictions, the proposed secret donation booth would not apply to organizations independent of candidates' control, groups like the Swift Boat Veterans for Truth or MoveOn.org, nor do Ackerman and Ayres propose instituting a cap on such donations. Donors could always direct funds there as a way to show support. To prove to Cheney that they love the GOP, for instance, hundreds of Big Oil executives might get together and publicly give $10 million to Americans for Good Things, a group that runs ads alleging that Democrats were secretly educated at madrassas. The oilmen would get to help Republicans *and* take credit for it.

Public and Private Money

Ackerman and Ayres have two responses to these worries. The first is that talk is cheap. The private assurances of donors might be comforting to a candidate, but Cheney could never really *trust* that the CEOs were telling him the truth—at least not as much as he trusts them now. And what if donors directed their funds to Swift Boat–style efforts? The professors say the key is to set tough rules to ensure that such groups really are independent of a candidate's control. And if that were the case, Cheney might not appreciate Big Oil's big donation to Americans for Good Things. He might feel slighted that it didn't deposit the money instead in the Bush campaign's coffers, where the money would have been much more useful to the campaign. Ackerman and Ayres add one more clever idea. If donations to independent groups rise by a substantial amount, then the FEC, under their plan, would correspondingly increase *public money* given in vouchers. In other words, by design, public money would always vastly outweigh private money, and ordinary people would always have more combined power than the wealthy.

By now this whole thing may sound quite technical, though it's actually far less complex than today's regime. In *Voting with Dollars*, their little-noticed 2004 book, Ackerman and Ayres outline their plan in great detail. They even include model legislation; Obama, Clinton or anyone else in Congress could introduce it tomorrow.

The Critics

That's not going to happen. And that's because there is one group that won't find this plan attractive: those already in power. Because the plan would make politics extremely unpredictable, incumbents are bound to see it as dangerous. The Right and some populists will reject using $6 billion or more in taxpayer money to finance campaigns—they'd call it welfare to politicians (though for less than the price of a month of war in Iraq, it's pretty cheap welfare). Others would rankle at the idea of keeping donations secret. Full disclosure has become so entrenched a part of our political lives that to abandon it might look insane. Another complaint might be that by adding more money to the system in the form of vouchers, candidates would simply launch bigger, noisier campaigns, though Ayres and Ackerman argue that the secret donation booth would cause a net decrease in private political money.

Still, what could be worse than today's laws? Many who are now vying for the White House have cast themselves as reformers. In announcing his bid, Obama lamented that politics has become "so gummed up by money and influence . . . that we can't tackle the big problems that demand solutions." Clinton's aides have suggested that she'd be in favor of overhauling today's presidential financing laws. The Ackerman-Ayres proposal is one plan that deserves serious consideration.

VIEWPOINT 8

> *"The [public financing] system was enacted for partisan gain, not for lofty public purposes."*

Public Financing of Presidential Campaigns Has Failed

John Samples

Public financing promotes partisan gain, not true reform, argues John Samples in the following viewpoint. The system was created following the resignation of President Richard Nixon to boost financial support for Democratic presidential candidates, he maintains. Since that time, incumbents from both parties have promoted campaign finance reforms that inhibit challengers, Samples claims. In fact, he asserts, the American public has little faith in the system, which is reflected in the low percentage of people who check off the public financing box on their tax returns. Samples, a Cato Institute scholar, is author of The Fallacy of Campaign Finance Reform.

John Samples, "Public-Financing Follies," *New York Post*, March 3, 2008.

As you read, consider the following questions:

1. What does John Samples claim is the irony of John McCain's and Barack Obama's support for campaign finance?
2. In the author's opinion, what is the consequence of McCain's being trapped in the public financing system?
3. Why is Obama eager to escape the public financing system, in the author's view?

America's decrepit and unpopular system of taxpayer financing of presidential campaigns has suddenly taken center stage in this year's [2008] election—with Sens. John McCain and Barack Obama each caught between his long-expressed principles and his self-interest.

McCain and Obama have long boasted of their support for aggressive regulation of money in politics. But now each would love to avoid taking public money. In that irony lies a lesson about campaign-finance "reform."

The Public-Funding Story

The presidential public-funding system dates to 1974, after President Richard Nixon resigned. At the time, Democrats held large majorities in Congress, but their presidential candidates faced serious funding challenges.

Since 1960, GOP presidential candidates had opened up a growing fund-raising lead over Democrats. If that trend had continued, Republican presidential candidates would be raising many times the sums raised by Democratic ones in 1976 and beyond. Public financing put an end to that threat.

The law offers equal sums to both major-party candidates for the fall campaign—so long as they don't raise money from private contributors. That imposed an equality of funding, stopping the growing GOP edge.

In other words, for all the talk of "reform" and corruption, regulations of campaign finance in fact are all about manipu-

Public Financing Is Dead

Sen. John McCain, an architect of sweeping campaign-finance reform who got walloped by a presidential candidate armed with more than $750 million, predicts that no one will ever again accept federal matching funds to run for the nation's highest office.

"No Republican in his or her right mind is going to agree to public financing. I mean, that's dead. That is over. The last candidate for president of the United States from a major party that will take public financing was me," [said McCain].

Joseph Curl and Stephen Dinan,
The Washington Times, *March 29, 2009.*

lating elections to boost specific interests. (In '74, it was Democrats in the presidential arena. Other "reform" laws have greatly benefited incumbents of both parties, at the expense of challengers. Still others, like recent New York City laws, boost labor unions' political power at the expense of businesses' [political power].)

The Realities of 2008

Back to the '08 race. Sen. McCain started his White House bid with private financing but ran out of cash last June [2007]. To keep going, he sought to qualify for public funding for the primary phase of the campaign—and used the possibility of such money as collateral for a loan.

That move got him through. McCain now is the sure GOP nominee. But it puts him in a bind as he looks toward the general election. If he's trapped in the public-funding system, he can spend only $4 million more between now [March

2008] and the Republican convention [September 2008]. That's far too little to keep his message before the public.

And it's a disaster for him. Barack Obama and Hillary Clinton have turned out to be extraordinary fund-raisers—and opted out of the public system for the primaries. If either captures the nomination soon, he or she can keep raising and spending private money all spring and summer long. McCain might well have lost the fall race before he receives more public money after the Republican convention.

Not surprising, McCain desperately wants out of the public system. (And since he hasn't actually received any public funds yet, he may be able to escape.)

Obama, meanwhile, is eager to escape the public system for the general election, the phase that begins after the conventions. He promised last year to take public financing if the GOP nominee did—but he's now learned that he could vastly out-raise McCain in the private sector.

The American public plainly shares this cynical view of our supposedly "clean" public-finance system. In recent years, only about 6 percent of federal tax fliers have checked off the box that directs $3 from their payment to the presidential campaign fund.

That's a 94–6 vote of no confidence in the system.

The system of public funding—and heavy regulation of private giving—for political candidates has its sincere defenders, people who believe democracy demands it.

But the facts speak for themselves. The system was enacted for partisan gain, not for lofty public purposes. And now two of its strongest supporters are looking to game the system—to escape public funding and rely on private cash—because it's in their clear self-interest.

It's time to end the wretched pretense that this system serves democracy.

Periodical Bibliography

The following articles have been selected to supplement the diverse views presented in this chapter.

Thomas J. Billitteri	"Campaign Finance Reform," *CQ Researcher*, June 13, 2008.
Emily Cadei	"Stretching the Reach of Soft Money," *CQ Weekly*, May 4, 2008.
Linda Greenhouse	"Justices Revisit Campaign Finance Issue," *The New York Times*, June 26, 2008.
Danielle Knight	"An Appeal for More Teeth: Is the Watchdog Too Tame?" *U.S. News & World Report*, September 24, 2007.
Alex Koppelman	"Supreme Court Rules 'Millionaire's Amendment' Unconstitutional," *Salon.com*, June 26, 2008.
Thomas E. Mann	"A Collapse of the Campaign Finance Regime?" *The Forum* [Brookings], April 2008.
Thomas E. Mann	"Suppressing Political Speech?" *Opportunity 08: What Matters* [Brookings], July 9, 2007.
Meredith McGehee	"Our Democracy Is Stronger with More Competition," *Roll Call*, October 9, 2008.
The New York Times	"Millionaires' Amendment," April 21, 2008.
Charlie Savage	"Campaign Finance Law Challenges," *The Boston Globe*, April 26, 2007.
Byron Shafer	"Has the U.S. Campaign Finance System Collapsed?" *The Forum*, 2008.
The Washington Post	"A Loophole Reopens," June 26, 2007.
George F. Will	"Paralyze the FEC? Splendid," *The Washington Post*, December 11, 2007.

CHAPTER 2

What Strategies Promote Fair Political Campaigns?

Chapter Preface

Whether judicial elections pose a serious threat to the impartiality of the courts is one of several controversies in the debate over which political campaign strategies promote fair political campaigns. The United States is one of only a few countries that require judges to face popular election. While federal judges, who serve life terms, are nominated by the president and confirmed by the Senate, in thirty-nine of fifty states, judges are elected. These elections can be partisan contests or retention elections, in which incumbents remain in office unless a majority votes to remove them. Until recently, judicial elections were not considered controversial. The increasing costs of judicial campaigns and the involvement of interest groups in these campaigns, however, has led some to question whether elected judges can remain impartial.

Those who support judicial election reform question the impartiality of elected judges. "Judicial elections are now posing the single, greatest threat to fair and impartial courts," argues Tommy Wells, president of the American Bar Association. These analysts argue that in some cases, donations to judicial campaigns might be tipping the scales of justice. One recent U.S. Supreme Court case on this issue is hailed by Bert Brandenburg of the liberal legal advocacy group Justice at Stake as a tremendous victory. In *Caperton v. Massey* (2009), the Court held that a West Virginia Supreme Court justice who overturned a $50 million jury award against a coal company violated the award recipient's constitutional rights to a fair hearing. The judge, they argued, should have recused himself from the case because an executive of the coal company had spent $3 million to elect him. "Courts are different from legislators and governors," Brandenburg maintains.

"Judges must make impartial decisions that are accountable to the law, not interest groups," he reasons.

Other analysts argue that judicial election reform is unnecessary. They maintain that for more than 150 years Americans have elected over 75 percent of trial judges and over 50 percent of appellate judges. "To indict judicial elections is to indict American justice generally," suggests Sean Parnell, president of the Center for Competitive Politics. He asserts that no evidence exists to suggest that elected judges have failed to uphold their oaths more than appointed judges do. "Whether or not a state relies on appointments or elections to fill its bench, there's no corruption inherent in either method," Parnell contends. Like-minded commentators claim that judges, particularly state supreme court judges, have the power to make law. Therefore, reasons lawyer James Bopp Jr., "It's only appropriate for the people to choose judges." These analysts question the Court's ruling in *Caperton*, arguing that the ruling in the case will lead to costly court cases based on unsubstantiated claims against judges. In his dissenting opinion, Chief Justice John Roberts writes, "The Court's new 'rule' . . . will inevitably lead to an increase in allegations that judges are biased, however groundless those charges may be."

Despite the outcome of *Caperton*, state legislators have shown little interest in changing the status quo. Indeed, advocates on both sides continue to debate whether judicial elections pose a threat to judicial impartiality. The authors in the following chapter debate the effectiveness of other strategies designed to promote fair political campaigns.

Viewpoint 1

> *"Only a system of public financing for congressional elections is capable of breaking the corrupting nexus of money and influence."*

Public Funding of Congressional Campaigns Will Promote Fair Political Campaigns

Ed Kilgore

In the following memo to President Barack Obama, Ed Kilgore of the Progressive Policy Institute argues that public financing of congressional campaigns will reduce private influence and increase accountability. As the cost of campaigns grows, so do campaign contributions from special-interest groups, which in turn feeds corruption and congressional gridlock, he asserts. U.S. Supreme Court decisions have weakened efforts to set congressional campaign finance limits, Kilgore maintains. Public funding of congressional campaigns is therefore necessary to offset the advantage of wealthier candidates, he reasons.

Ed Kilgore, "Reforming Congressional Elections," Progressive Policy Institute, January 15, 2009. Reproduced by permission.

As you read, consider the following questions:

1. According to Ed Kilgore, how will a campaign finance reform offensive help President Barack Obama's party?
2. In addition to public financing, how does the bill sponsored by Senators Richard Durbin and Arlen Specter promote fair campaigns, in the author's view?
3. How would the proposal sponsored by Al Gore clean up campaigns, in the author's opinion?

If the 2008 campaign produced any clear and unambiguous mandate from the American people, it is for fundamental change in Washington. Regardless of their presidential preference, a majority of voters share a profound sense of disgust with small-minded partisanship, special-interest obstructionism, and the power of lobbyists to subvert the common good.

A Clear Opportunity

This convergence of demands for change, across the usual partisan and ideological lines, provides you one clear opportunity to overcome the record of the last eight years—and the one distinct path to everything else you want to accomplish. That is why I urge you to make "changing Washington" your first priority as president.

Obviously, you have many urgent challenges competing for your time and attention: bringing the war in Iraq to an acceptable conclusion, turning around our economy, and a hundred other things. But rallying public support for a dramatic change in Washington's political culture will help you mobilize support for every other step you take, and it will improve the chances for progress on substantive reforms.

Specifically, you should signal your continuing commitment to clean campaigns and to the goal of breaking the power of lobbyists over Washington. By calling for voluntary public financing of congressional campaigns you would slow or even stop the revolving door that now so easily whisks legislative and executive personnel from public decision-making to private decision-influencing.

Such a direct assault on "politics as usual" will preempt the otherwise inevitable media story line that you, like past presidents, are putting aside campaign rhetoric in order to adjust to the realities of power in Washington—a point of view guaranteed to disappoint the public and undermine your postelection momentum.

Any reform initiative must, of course, be tangible to be credible. [An] attack on how lawmakers perpetuate their own power at the expense of the common good is the best and most audacious avenue to pursue.

Public Financing of Congressional Campaigns

With Congress's approval ratings at an all-time low, a reform offensive will also enable members of your party to make a fresh start, while providing members from the other party with an earlier test of their commitment to the reform ethic so many embraced during the 2008 campaign.

Without question, special-interest campaign contributions are the mother's milk of corruption, obstructionism, and gridlock in Congress. As the cost of political campaigns has grown exponentially, the dependence of congressional candidates on special-interest dollars has grown as well.

This year, the most direct and formal method of special-interest fund-raising—political action committees (PACs)—contributed about $4 of every $10 raised by House candidates, and about one-third of all dollars raised by Senate candidates (the numbers were significantly higher for congressional incumbents running for reelection).

Special-interest domination of party-committee and independent-advocacy donations (including the increasingly important infusions of cash from the so-called "527s") was

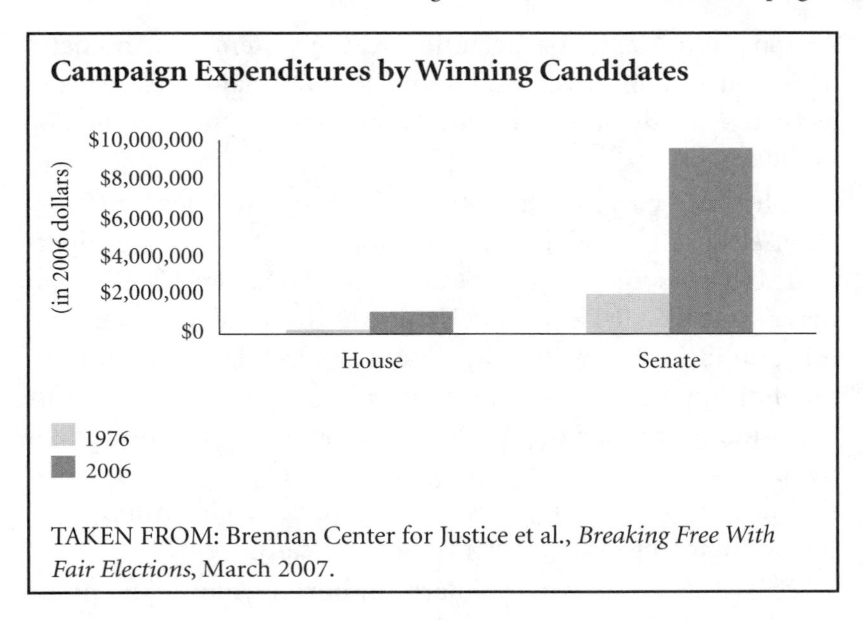

Campaign Expenditures by Winning Candidates

TAKEN FROM: Brennan Center for Justice et al., *Breaking Free With Fair Elections*, March 2007.

significantly larger. Moreover, the widespread practice of "bundling" made it increasingly possible to link batches of individual contributions to particular interests or causes. When you factor in the estimated $2.8 billion spent on congressional lobbying activities last year [2008] alone, it comes to approximately $5 million per member of Congress.

Recent Supreme Court decisions have weakened earlier congressional attempts to set contribution and expenditure limits. Only a system of public financing for congressional elections is capable of breaking the corrupting nexus of money and influence.

The "Clean Money/Clean Elections" Model

While a variety of models for voluntary public financing have been advanced over the years, the "clean money/clean elections" model, offering direct candidate subsidies in exchange for strict expenditure limits, is the best available today. Seven states have enacted variations on this proposal. In the two states with the most comprehensive public-financing systems,

Arizona and Maine, participation in the system by candidates has risen steadily over time, with sizable majorities of state legislative candidates in both states choosing public financing in 2006.

The best current legislation adapting the "clean money/ clean elections" model to congressional elections is the bipartisan bill co-sponsored by Sens. Richard Durbin (D-Ill.) and Arlen Specter (R-Pa.). Aside from the basic idea of offering full public financing to congressional candidates agreeing to expenditure limits, this bill also provides discounted broadcast television ad rates, along with "fair fight" funds to offset independent expenditure campaigns—thus closing (or at least shrinking) one of the largest loopholes undermining the public-financing system for presidential campaigns.

This last point is particularly important, given the arguments that broke out during the campaign over the presidential public-financing system. It is time to acknowledge that the presidential system has been broken by outdated spending limits and the independent-expenditure loophole. Bipartisan legislation from Sens. Russ Feingold (D-Wis.) and Susan Collins (R-Maine) would fix these problems, and merits your support.

Some campaign-finance reformers this last year raised hopes that Internet-based small donations might represent an alternative form of public financing. That may be true, but the "small-donor revolution" remains a distant rumor in congressional campaigns: This year, fewer than 10 percent of all congressional contributions were made in amounts under $200.

In any event, voluntary public financing and small-donor fund-raising are complementary, not mutually exclusive. Any congressional public-financing model could exempt very small contributions, and any candidate opting out of public financing in order to raise money exclusively from such donations could be deemed "clean."

Here is another variation on the clean campaign theme, based on a creative proposal Al Gore made during the 2000 presidential campaign: Instead of making contributions directly to candidates, individuals would have the option of donating money to a new Democracy Endowment that would finance congressional campaigns. They would receive a tax credit for every dollar they contribute to the Endowment. Candidates would qualify for money if they agreed not to accept any other sources of funding and to limit their overall campaign spending.

To offset the advantage of rich candidates who finance their own campaigns, the Endowment's managers could make sure that participating candidates have enough funding to be competitive. This indirect system of public financing would be entirely voluntary and as such would not raise any constitutional issues.

Whatever approach to reform you choose, the important thing is to demonstrate your resolve to sever the link between public legislation and private campaign donations.

Viewpoint 2

> *"Campaign finance limits and taxpayer-funded elections will not clean up state government. They will not reduce the influence of special interest groups."*

Public Funding of Congressional Campaigns Will Not Promote Fair Political Campaigns

Nathan Benefield

Public financing of congressional campaigns will not make elections more fair, argues Nathan Benefield in the following viewpoint. In fact, he asserts, campaign finance regulations curb political speech and protect incumbents. Indeed, limits make it more difficult for people to obtain information about the candidates, Benefield claims. The public has greater access to candidates who appeal to a broad group of supporters than to candidates limited by public financing, he reasons. Benefield is director of policy research with the Commonwealth Foundation. This viewpoint is taken from his testimony before the Pennsylvania House of Representatives regarding Pennsylvania House Bills (HB) 1497 and 1720.

Nathan Benefield, "Campaign Finance 'Reform' Is a Wolf in Sheep's Clothing," common wealthfoundation.org, August 14, 2007. Reproduced by permission.

As you read, consider the following questions:

1. According to Nathan Benefield, how much more do large companies such as Microsoft spend on advertising than a typical presidential candidate spends on his or her campaign?
2. What evidence does the author provide that federal campaign finance laws have not cleaned up national politics?
3. In the author's view, what did New Jersey's 2005 gubernatorial campaign reveal about public financing?

While we [the scholars of the Commonwealth Foundation, a public policy think tank] commend the intent of . . . offering serious attempts to deliver much-needed reforms to state government, we believe that expanding the power of elected and appointed officials to control campaign funding will not have the desired effects.

Limiting campaign contributions and putting election finance under government control only serves to protect incumbents from challengers. Those with name recognition—and under HB 1497, ties to government agents—benefit when we curb the free speech of their opponents. The power to fund or silence speech about candidates will certainly be abused by those who benefit and control the system.

The Primary Justifications

There are two primary justifications used to support campaign finance laws such as these—that there is "too much money in politics" and that special interests have too much influence under current campaign finance laws.

There have been a number of recent news stories that mention the high costs of elections—these stories usually mention the 2008 presidential election will cost over $1 billion for all candidates. Is this too much money? Let me suggest that it is not even close. Though much of this money goes to staff and travel, mostly it is advertising, as the campaign is advertising a candidate. But this amount is relatively small in comparison with corporate advertising spending. The top spending presidential candidate may spend $400 million over 20 months of campaigning. In 2003 (which likely understates current spending, but illustrates the point nonetheless), General Motors spent $3.43 billion in advertising, Procter & Gamble spent $3.23 billion, and Time Warner spent $3.1 billion. This list of the top 25 companies ends with Microsoft, which spent $1.15 billion.

Each of these companies spends more than twice in advertising than the cost of any presidential candidate's entire campaign. So I don't believe we can say there is too much money flowing into political campaigns. I want to know more about a potential leader of the free world—or about a potential governor, or even a school board member—than I do about the side effects of Viagra. Campaign finance limits restrict the public's ability to get more information about candidates, and undermine the deliberative process.

Concerns About Special Interests

Second, the concern about special interests is warranted, but does not justify either piece of legislation under consideration. These bills are designed to prevent wealthy individuals and special interest PACs [political action committees] from controlling who gets money for campaign expenditures. It would replace them with government bureaucrats and legislators determining who and how individuals get campaign funds. Many advocates of campaign finance reform mistrust wealthy individuals, along with special interest PACs, and want to limit their influence. But just as many, including the Commonwealth Foundation, are equally mistrustful of government bureaucrats and legislators, and fear legislation to expand their influence, while limiting that of the private sector.

No Evidence That Public Funding Works

Our privately funded system has the virtue of requiring candidates to compete in the marketplace of ideas for contributions. Public funding requires mindless subsidies for failed ideas that might be better relegated to the dustbin of history.

The belief that public funding will somehow clean up our election system is based on rhetoric, not facts. Evidence that contributions substantially influence votes is almost nonexistent.

Hans A. von Spakovsky, Politico, *April 3, 2009.*

Under current law, individuals are free to support (or not support) candidates of their choosing. They can contribute to the candidate they feel best represents their views, or the candidate they think is most likely to win, or merely a friend.

Certainly this system presents opportunities for corruption. Candidates and donors may enter into a quid pro quo (even though this is currently banned by law)—promising to exchange future votes or favors for campaign donations. Donors may also try to buy access or "face time" with a candidate.

But candidates today have to find multiple donors to their campaign. They have to find supporters from different walks of life, different businesses, and different interests. This balancing act requires them to appeal to a broad array of supporters, and not be obliged to a single individual or group. This ensures that candidates have a broad public appeal, and are not simply propped up by a government program gone awry.

Limiting Public Access to Information

Under government financed campaigns, such as those proposed under HB 1497, candidates only have to appeal to one funding source. And individuals have no choice about who they will support—their taxes will be used to finance the campaigns chosen by law and by a government agency. Instead of needing to appeal to a broad group of supporters, candidates only need to get support from those who control the system.

Candidates are also currently required to disclose their list of donors, allowing the public, media, and watchdog groups to see who their supporters are. With donation limits, contributors will simply funnel money through additional PACs, or donate in the name of friends, to get around this limit. This will result in less information being made available.

Campaign contribution limits will reinforce the advantages incumbents have in name recognition, staff, media exposure, and office budgets—particularly when taxpayers fund "public service announcements" and mailing of calendars with incumbents' names and pictures. Campaign limits also benefit those who start early—which quite clearly favors incumbents, given the number of fund-raisers held in Harrisburg [the capital of Pennsylvania] by General Assembly members, which are held from beginning to end of the two-year legislative session.

Furthermore, campaign finance laws such as these have failed to deliver their promised benefits. Consider federal campaign finance contribution limits, similar to those as HB 1720 would create. Campaign contribution limits have not "cleaned up" national politics. Public approval of Congress is lower than ever. Congress is plagued by scandals, earmarks, and corruption. And there is little evidence that "special interests" have less influence.

Contribution limits undoubtedly hindered efforts by minor party and independent candidates. The exceptions being those who bankroll their own campaign, such as Ross Perot, as federal and state laws cannot limit individuals from supporting their own candidacy.

Sheltering Incumbents

And instead of making elections more competitive, incumbent congressmen have become more shielded. Since campaign finance limits were passed . . . less than 2% of incumbents [lost] elections. Retirements, death, and even indictment account for more turnover in Congress. Taxpayer-financed campaigns, such as those proposed under HB 1497, have even worse track records. The number of individuals participating in the Presidential Campaign [Election] Fund has been declining every year. In 2004 only 9.2% of taxpayers elected to contribute to this fund, contrasted with 28.7% in 1980—indicating voters are becoming dissatisfied with this system. Even though contributing to the Presidential Campaign [Election] Fund only requires checking a box on a tax return, and only costs $3, more than twice as many people contribute to individual presidential campaigns, and in amounts far exceeding $3. I can only conclude that voters would rather spend their own money than have government spend it for them.

Arizona's public financing of elections has not had the desired effect either. Since the "Clean Elections Law" was passed in 1998, the incumbent success rate increased. The number of candidates for office has declined. And Arizona voters have far more information about privately funded campaigns than about "Clean Election" candidates.

Finally, [Pennsylvania representative Greg] Vitali has stated the HB 1497 is based on New Jersey's system of publicly financing gubernatorial elections. It should be noted that [New Jersey governor Jon] Corzine refused to participate in the publicly financed system in 2005, spending $43 million of his own money instead. His chief opponent also bankrolled his own campaign, spending tens of millions of his own money.

If the goal of this legislation is to ensure a race between multimillionaire and multimillionaire, I promise you, it will succeed.

Campaign finance limits and taxpayer-funded elections will not clean up state government. They will not reduce the influence of special interest groups. They will not create greater accountability.

These laws may disguise corruption, and they may result in less information being available about the influence of special interests. They are likely to decrease public confidence in government and participation in elections.

Finally, we are concerned that campaign finance laws like these will serve to protect incumbents from criticism during their reelection campaigns, and will limit the ability of their challengers and other groups from getting their messages heard—effectively denying freedom of speech for the most critical type of speech of all: political speech.

Viewpoint 3

> *"Attack ads . . . have twisted the truth, lied about personal background, taken statements out of context, and clearly sought to manipulate voter sentiments."*

Attack Ads That Go Beyond the Issues Undermine Fair Political Campaigns

Darrell M. West

When negative attack ads are deceptive, they undermine the political process, claims Darrell M. West in the following viewpoint. Attack ads that focus on the issues are appropriate and inevitable, he concedes. Misleading ads that twist the truth, lie about candidates, or take statements out of context, however, threaten the electoral system. Unfortunately, he concludes, efforts to mislead voters in the 2008 presidential election made it clear that voters themselves must be vigilant to get to the truth. West, of the Brookings Institution, is author of Air Wars: Television Advertising in Election Campaigns, 1952–2004.

As you read, consider the following questions:

1. What historical campaigns does Darrell M. West cite as evidence that attack ads have a long history?

Darrell M. West, "2008 Campaign Attack Ads Hit an All-Time Low," CNN.com, September 15, 2008. Reproduced by permission.

2. How does the author say voters can protect themselves against political manipulation?
3. What percentage of the campaign budget do presidential candidates spend on ads, according to the author?

Negative attacks are as American as apple pie. Since the early days of the republic, candidates attacked with a vigor that contemporary strategists would admire.

In the 1800 presidential election, for example, Thomas Jefferson and John Adams criticized one another with a stunning ferocity on everything from foreign and domestic policy to private character and personal behavior.

Later campaigns weren't much better. Critics of Andrew Jackson in 1836 accused him of murdering Indians. In 1884, Grover Cleveland was ridiculed for fathering an illegitimate child. William Jennings Bryan was characterized as a dangerous radical in 1896 who would ruin the economy.

Reaching All-Time Lows

Despite these historical precedents, the 2008 campaign has reached all-time lows in the use of misleading and inaccurate political appeals. Even Karl Rove, the architect of negative ads in previous campaigns, has complained about the tenor of this year's campaign.

John McCain broadcast an ad taking Barack Obama's words out of context and suggesting Democrats were trying to compare GOP vice presidential nominee Sarah Palin to a pig. The McCain campaign ran another spot erroneously claiming Obama favored comprehensive sex education for kindergarteners.

Democrats have not been above reproach either. After McCain secured the GOP nomination this spring, outside groups falsely claimed the Republican supported a 1,000-year war in Iraq and therefore was not worthy of the presidency.

Do Negative Campaign Ads Work?

- 59% [of those surveyed by the Project on Campaign Conduct] believe that all or most candidates deliberately twist the truth.
- 39% believe that all or most candidates deliberately lie to voters.
- 43% believe that most or all candidates deliberately make unfair attacks on their opponents. Another 45% believe that some candidates do.
- 67% say they can trust the government in Washington only some of the time or never.
- 87% are concerned about the level of personal attacks in today's political campaigns.

ThisNation.com, *2008. www.thisnation.com.*

These misleading appeals suggest voters must remain vigilant about candidate, party, and group claims. Generally, the most misleading commercials have come from independent groups uncoordinated with the candidates.

These organizations feel free to run emotional and inaccurate content designed to play on voters' fears and anxieties. Some of the worst ads in recent memory, such as the Willie Horton ad in 1988[1], have been broadcast by these kinds of groups.

In past years, the only upside of attack ads was that they generally contained more issue content than other types of

1. In the 1988 U.S. presidential race, a political ad criticized candidate Michael Dukakis, then governor of Massachusetts, for support of a prison weekend furlough program that released Willie Horton, a convicted felon serving a life sentence for murder. During his release, Horton committed armed robbery and rape.

ads. Since reporters police campaign appeals, the ads generally stick to the issues and rely on factually-accurate information. Ad sponsors and candidates realize they will be held accountable for unfair ad content.

A New Pattern

However, commercials run this year [2008] represent a break with this general pattern. Attack ads broadcast in recent months have twisted the truth, lied about personal background, taken statements out of context, and clearly sought to manipulate voter sentiments.

Most worrisome from a factual standpoint is McCain's claim that Obama will raise taxes on the middle class. Although Obama has pledged to increase income taxes on those earning more than $250,000, he has been careful not to make proposals that would raise taxes on the middle class for fear of being labeled a tax-and-spend liberal.

McCain's tax claims have been condemned by leading editorial boards and surely will attract considerable attention in upcoming debates.

With all the factual inaccuracies that have taken place, voters need to protect themselves from efforts at political manipulation. Nonpartisan Web sites such as www.factcheck.org represent one source of unbiased information. They analyze ads and compile factual information in support of or in opposition to ad claims.

Other trustworthy fact-checkers include ad watches and reality checks run by leading news organizations. These features dissect candidate claims in regard to accuracy, strategy, and impact.

But the best thing for voters to do is to watch the candidate debates and judge for themselves. Study the statements and the factual bases of policy claims. Pay attention to how the candidates speak and what they say. Find out what nonpartisan groups think and see what they have to say regarding the major issues.

By the time the campaign is over, the presidential candidates are expected to have spent 55 percent of their overall budget on ads. Strategists put together spots very carefully and pre-test major messages on small groups of voters.

Most of this money will be devoted to television spots. But increasing amounts are being targeted on radio, direct mail, and Internet appeals.

In the end, voters are going to have to decipher competing charges and counter-charges amid considerable noise from all sides. The 2008 election is unusual in having so many big issues on the agenda: the economy, the Iraq and Afghanistan wars, health care, taxes, immigration, education and climate change.

It is an election that truly matters because of the stark differences between the parties and the closeness of the campaign. Voters need to pay serious attention to the facts in order to make a wise choice.

VIEWPOINT 4

"Attack ads aren't just inevitable; they're actually helpful to voters."

Negative Campaign Ads Play an Important Role in Political Campaigns

John G. Geer

Attack ads actually help voters make more informed choices than positive ads, argues John G. Geer in the following viewpoint. Negative ads are more likely to address the issues of the day. Moreover, Geer claims, negative ads often contain more facts. While political candidates are very good at telling voters about what they do well, attack ads address their weaknesses, he reasons. Geer, a professor at Vanderbilt University, is author of In Defense of Negativity: Attack Ads in Presidential Campaigns.

As you read, consider the following questions:

1. In John G. Geer's opinion, why did John McCain take an aggressive tone near the end of his presidential campaign?
2. Why does the author believe that ads pointing to John Kerry's voting record on taxes were not hitting below the belt?

John G. Geer, "Those Negative Ads Are a Positive Thing," *Washington Post*, October 12, 2008.

3. In the author's view, why are so many people aware of the term "Swift Boat"?

It's that time again. With the mud flying in the [2008] presidential race, pundits, journalists and political observers of all stripes are denouncing the campaign's new, strikingly negative tone. Listening to them, you'd think that the very fabric of our democracy was being ripped apart every time a candidate aired a tough attack ad, threw an elbow or issued a sharply worded statement. It's no surprise that the public has joined the chorus to denounce negativity in politics. But as someone who has spent years studying negative advertising, I say hold the handwringing over attack ads. They're actually pretty good for the country.

Straight Talk About Attack Ads

Before you [express] disgust at my heresy, let me offer, as Sen. John McCain likes to say, some "straight talk." For starters, let's not be prudish about this. Really, what did we expect to happen? The polls all show that Sen. Barack Obama has opened up a significant lead over McCain, who is saddled with a sagging economy and a wildly unpopular president. Senior GOP operatives recently told *The Washington Post* that the McCain campaign would take a newly aggressive tone to try "to change the subject here," as one McCain hand put it. So is it any wonder that McCain is airing mostly negative ads at this point?

And Obama's not innocent, either. While McCain's running mate, Gov. Sarah Palin, blasted the Democratic nominee for his rather thin ties to a seemingly unrepentant member of the Vietnam-era Weather Underground, Obama responded with an ad reminding voters of McCain's role in the "Keating Five" savings and loan scandal of the 1980s. Recent data from Nielsen suggest that the campaigns have aired roughly the same number of negative ads. Even Karl Rove, who knows a thing or two about attack ads, has declared that both sides have gone too negative.

Attack Ads Are More Informative

Most people assume that negativity in politics is a bad thing. But they're wrong. Attack ads aren't just inevitable; they're actually helpful to voters. Negative ads, on average, are actually more informative than positive ones. This claim sounds like sacrilege in light of all the negativity about negativity, but the data are clear. Believe it or not, I've examined all the ads aired by presidential candidates on television from 1960 to 2004, and my analysis has led me to some startling conclusions:

First, negative ads are more likely than positive ads to be about the issues.

Second, negative ads are more likely to be specific when talking about those issues.

Third, negative ads are more likely to contain facts.

And finally, negative ads are more likely to be about the important issues of the day.

How is this possible? How can something so widely reviled actually turn out to be good for us? It's like finding out that Big Macs are nutritious.

Why Attack Ads Work

The problem is that we rarely consider what's necessary for a negative ad to work. Obama can't just say that a McCain presidency would be bad for the economy. Instead, he must make an argument, even a 30-second one, showing how McCain's policies will supposedly lead to an economic downturn. That forces Obama to be much more specific than he is when he's out on the stump touting his own vague desire to grow the economy.

Moreover, attacks need evidence to work. Could Obama attack McCain as unprepared to serve as commander-in-chief?

Not in this lifetime. McCain has the necessary experience, and claiming otherwise would backfire. Similarly, McCain can't question Obama's intelligence because the Democrat is clearly smart. When ads lack the evidence to support their claims, they tend to work against the candidate who aired them. Just consider the flak McCain took recently after running his "sex education" ad. It simply wasn't credible to claim that Obama supported sex education for 6-year-old kids.

Part of the reason people don't like negative ads is that attacks aren't fun; learning about someone's weaknesses isn't enjoyable. Nonetheless, it's important. In 1988, for example, then vice president George H.W. Bush's campaign was criticized for airing the famous "tank ad," which used footage of a helmet-wearing Michael S. Dukakis driving around in a tank while the narrator listed defense programs that the Massachusetts governor opposed. Sure, the video made Dukakis look like Snoopy, but the ad also raised important themes for voters. With the Cold War raging, the public needed to know about the candidates' views on defense policy. If you listened only to Dukakis's own ads, you would have thought that he was a bigger supporter of defense than Bush. But the record suggested otherwise.

That ad was an important corrective to the overly generous account candidates usually offer about their own records. In 2004, Sen. John F. Kerry described himself as someone who supported tax cuts. The Bush campaign had to point out the many times Kerry had supported tax increases. Is that hitting below the belt? Hardly. The public needed to know Kerry's full record on taxes. Kerry never would have provided it—but the negative ads did.

The bottom line: Candidates are great at telling us all about their strengths, but they just won't tell us about their weaknesses. So that task falls to their opponents. We need this negative information to make an informed choice.

Attack Ads Spark Public Interest

Political attack ads, widely demonized by pundits and politicians, are instead a kind of multivitamin for the democratic process, sparking voters' interest and participation. . . .

"There's this gut reaction that if a political advertisement is negative, it must have a deleterious affect on American politics," says [political scientist Kenneth] Goldstein. "Contrary to conventional wisdom, the more that people are exposed to negative advertising, the more they know, the more engaged they are and the more likely they are to vote."

Dennis Chaptman,
"Negative Campaign Ads Contribute to a Healthy Democracy, Political Scientist Argues," University of Wisconsin - Madison Online, *January 14, 2008. www.wisc.edu.*

Explaining What's Wrong with Those in Charge

I'll push my own Straight Talk Express even further: Any democracy *demands* negativity. Our nation rests on the idea that ordinary citizens can replace one set of leaders with another. But to make that change, we need those out of power to explain what's wrong with those in charge. The beauty of our system is the peaceful transfer of power, and that absolutely requires negativity.

Some may say that purely negative campaigns undermine this country and produce nothing of value. Perhaps. But if you want to see some truly "negative" campaigns, forget 2008 or 1988 and go back to the founding of the republic. First, consider the Declaration of Independence—one of our most hallowed documents. It is also strikingly negative, attacking King George's actions toward the colonies. Or consider the debate over the adoption of the Constitution. Its foes waged a harsh, nasty and sometimes personal campaign against the Federalists and our new founding charter. By one estimate, 90 percent of all the anti-Federalists' statements were attacks on the Constitution. The result of all this negativity? The Bill of Rights—not a bad outcome at all.

Not every attack this season has been a good thing, of course. The number of attack ads seems excessive to me, too. We're usually told that all these negative commercials are aired because they work. But that doesn't hold water. Despite that conventional wisdom, there's no systematic evidence that attack ads work better than positive ones. We can all point to famous negative ads that seemed to swing an election, but the same can be said of positive ads. Remember Ronald Reagan's beautiful "Morning in America" ads, which laid out the many successes of Reagan's first term? Walter Mondale sure does.

The Media's Love for Attack Ads

The reason we have so many negative ads in 2008 has less to do with their efficacy or virtue than with the way the media cover campaigns. Today's coverage gives candidates far more incentive to run negative ads than they had 20 or 30 years ago. Consultants know that reporters and bloggers love harsh, negative ads. Journalists relish the battle and revel in the attacks. When was the last time you saw a news story about a positive ad? I recently asked a panel of journalists this question, and only Joe Klein of *TIME* magazine could say that he had recently written about one of Obama's more uplifting ads. The sugary stuff may work with voters, but it doesn't set journalists' and pundits' pulses racing.

Hence this cycle has seen an increase in nasty ads online and lots of negative spots airing in just a few media markets. The campaigns are, in effect, fishing: dropping a lot of lines in the water in hopes of hooking the media. Take all the attention the McCain team's "Celebrity" ad received earlier this year [2008] by linking Obama to Paris Hilton and Britney Spears. This ad was clever, and it offered a theme that the media found interesting and relevant: Is Obama ready to lead?

But the best, and most troubling, illustration comes from the 2004 presidential race. We all know the term "Swift Boat," but not because many of us saw the actual ad that ripped Kerry's Vietnam service. The ad didn't get much air time, but the media lavished attention on the controversial spot. I did a systematic search of media coverage from August to November 2004 and found that the term "Swift Boat" got nearly twice as many mentions in major U.S. newspapers as the term "Iraq war."

All this straight talk may be received with, well, some negativity. As a defender of negativity, I can only say: Bring it on. We need to continually evaluate, judge and criticize our ideas, and that means we need negativity. It plays an important role in letting the country decide who's ready to lead. It may not be pretty, but democratic politics rarely are. U.S. elections are pitched battles for control of the federal government. The stakes are huge, and tempers flare. But the candidate left standing will be battle-tested for the fiery trial that awaits him when he takes that oath of office.

VIEWPOINT 5

> *"Thanks to the . . . airing of false advertising and broadcaster retreat from journalistic responsibilities, the American people are denied the fundamental democratic principle of free and fair elections."*

Media Regulation Is Necessary to Promote Fair Political Campaigns

Sarah O'Leary

The agencies designed to regulate the media have failed to protect American voters from media manipulation, maintains Sarah O'Leary in the following viewpoint. In the past, journalists were willing to offend politicians to ask the day's tough questions, but today's journalists are more interested in maintaining access, she claims. In fact, O'Leary argues, today's broadcast journalists report false political attacks without pointing out the facts, thus becoming a forum for propaganda. Without guidance, a deregulated media will manipulate rather than inform the American public, she reasons. O'Leary, a regular contributor for The Huffington Post, *is a well-known marketing expert.*

Sarah O'Leary, "Deregulated Media and Our Endless Campaign 'Silly Season,'" *The Huffington Post*, September 23, 2008.

As you read, consider the following questions:

1. According to Sarah O'Leary, how has the Federal Communications Commission (FCC) ignored its primary function?
2. Why has the Federal Trade Commission (FTC) refused to become involved in political advertising, in the author's opinion?
3. What famous broadcaster does the author cite as one who understood the weighty responsibility of broadcast journalists?

As a democracy, the U.S. government guarantees us the right to "free and fair" elections. Ideally, every licensed voter can cast a ballot without fear of harm or reprisal, and all votes are counted. But this certainly isn't all that there is to a free and fair election. Our government, through the unconscionable complacency of the deregulated Federal Communications Commission (FCC), the Federal Election Commission (FEC), the Federal Trade Commission (FTC) and Congress, has derailed our right to fair elections well before we pull the curtain to cast our votes. The roles played by broadcasters and political advertisers in the months leading up to the first Tuesday in November are critical to the legitimate execution of our political process. Thanks to the blatant and careless airing of false advertising and broadcaster retreat from journalistic responsibilities, the American people are denied the fundamental democratic principle of free and fair elections. If citizens are fed half-truths and lies, the outcome of the election process certainly cannot be considered fair.

A Climate of Misrepresentation

Refusing to intercede as a protectorate of the airwaves, a seemingly powerless FCC has ignored its primary function as the people's advocate within the realm of pubic broadcasting, fall-

ing desperately short of its mandated duties. By choosing not to enforce the governmental mandates designed to guide broadcasters while protecting the American people, the FCC's ineptness has afforded a climate of misrepresentation on the airwaves.

All licensed broadcasters must act "in the interest, convenience and necessity" of the American people as outlined by the commission or risk losing their licenses. (The American people own the airwaves and broadcasters merely lease access, with the FCC standing as the federal governor of such licenses.) By knowingly airing false political advertising and carrying news stories that would not stand up to the litmus test of truth, broadcasters are doing a fundamental disservice to the American people. Although a deregulated FCC washes its hands of responsibility by asserting local communities should be the truth police of the political airwaves, it is ludicrous to put the onus on them. Citizens are not equipped to battle broadcasters, nor can they fully participate in fair elections if what is being conveyed to them by broadcasters is false or misleading. The broadcasters have a duty to question, not simply accept, the information provided to them and the political ads they voluntarily air.

In recent years, broadcasters seem more afraid of politicians blocking access to candidates and stories than the potential threat of a deregulated FCC's censures. Without the story provided by the candidate, the broadcaster risks losing market share and with it advertising revenue. Looking to societal trends rather than delivering what is best for the citizen, broadcasters have swung the content pendulum to the tabloid rather than the informative. We are told about up-dos before issues, erroneous mud slinging rather than policy driven fact. Without the FCC demanding otherwise, broadcasters have little impetus for change. Further, a media focused on staying on the good side of politicians in exchange for access falls prey to the most dangerous of pitfalls—media manipulation.

The pit bull watchdog of consumer advertising, the FTC, sits the political advertising dance out because it claims no product is being sold. In the 22 years I've been in marketing, I can't think of a larger, more carefully packaged product being sold to the American people than that of the office of the President of the United States. Campaigns sell personalities and concepts and ideas to a voting American public. Millions of Americans donate money to campaigns that they learn of from broadcasters, making the argument that there's no money in the game baseless. If the FTC would simply extend its non-political advertising regulations to that of political advertising, the face of such communication would be drastically transformed.

Abdicating Its Responsibility to the American People

Beyond political advertising, TV and radio stations have often forgotten that the higher purpose of broadcast journalism is to factually inform the American people about the political issues facing the country. Broadcasters are advocates of the people, charged with acting in their best interests first and foremost. Reporting on political candidate fashion trends and filling the airwaves with who didn't really call whom a pig or other forms of political saber rattling disguised as fact dangerously erode a critical bond between broadcaster and audience. Edward R. Morrow, the patriarch of broadcast journalism, once interviewed an empty chair on the news show "See It Now" when Senator Joseph McCarthy refused an invitation to speak on the issues. Willing to ask the tough questions on behalf of the American people, Murrow's actions led to the eventual demise of the corrupt senator. Mr. Murrow understood the weighty responsibility he had to the American people and acted in our "interest, convenience and necessity."

There's a psychological term when a patient is running from his/her issues called "avoidance." The therapist searches for what it is a patient doesn't want to address rather than simply accept at face value the misdirection. In this campaign cycle, broadcasters often seem more interested in the sensational rather than the substance, not looking to what politicians hoping to distract are so desperate to avoid. It is a broadcaster's responsibility, however, to deliver to the American public the truth in the best way they know as professionals to do. Otherwise, the broadcaster falls victim to masterful media manipulation.

If a candidate would prefer not to speak to the issues, his or her camp can wipe out a day of reporting by falsely attacking a rival. The sensational attack will serve two purposes: 1) it will divert attention from the issues the public deserves to have addressed and 2) once reported, the audience may believe the lie to be true. Broadcast journalists have a responsibility not only for fact, but also for substance. It is to execute blinders on reporting that is devoid of real fact checking. The airwaves aren't meant to be a forum for propaganda, but for honesty. And the big loser is not the unfairly defeated candidate, but the American people.

Knowingly Spreading False Information

In the Communications Act of 1934 (as amended by the Telecommunications Act of 1996), the FCC itself stated that a broadcaster could lose its license if it "has knowingly transmitted false or deceptive signals or communications." The FCC is well aware that licensees are not supposed to propagate misrepresentations, but seems disinterested in pursuing such situations in regards to political reporting or advertising. The FCC is clear that censorship by broadcasters of candidates is forbidden, yet rarely holds the broadcaster responsible for derailing the spread of propaganda.

At one point in media time, there was grave concern about subliminal advertising, or messages covertly planted within advertising unbeknownst to the viewer or listener. The government swiftly outlawed such communication, as such obvious manipulation was most certainly not in the citizens' best interest. At present, there's no need for subliminal political advertising. Thanks to the ineffectiveness of the FCC and FTC, politicians and action groups can spread untruths in full view on news programs and through advertising for all to see without any negative repercussions.

We couldn't have learned this lesson more fully than we did with the now infamous reporting of Iraq's weapons of mass destruction.[1] The results of such misinformation, widely distributed by a mostly unquestioning media, have been world changing. If we allow the same principles of misdirection to be applied to the race for the most important political office in the world, we risk having the American people make deci-

1. The assertion by the George W. Bush administration that Iraq possessed weapons of mass destruction—later shown to be false—was a major justification for the 2003 U.S.-led invasion of Iraq.

sions based on airwave truth-lies; statements that are broadcast through formats that we trust to deliver factual information to us.

Deregulation Is to Blame

The deregulation of the FCC, particularly under President [Ronald] Reagan in the mid-80s, must shoulder the lion's share of blame when considering the ineptness of today's commission. Tragically, without federal governance of our airwaves, we create a sieve-like system that gives too many opportunities for skillful audience manipulation. How does a local community control a national network? It simply cannot. Believing that the communities and its citizens can police airwaves is simply an excuse for inaction, and certainly not in keeping with the wants, needs and desires of the American public.

Experts in marketing and media will attest that we're in the midst of a cycle of media manipulation that surpasses any other time in our country's history. The American people deserve truth on the airwaves, and the FCC should be revoking the licenses of stations that knowingly distribute misinformation. The job of our government and the broadcasters who use public airwaves is to serve their citizens.

With an economy on the brink of a catastrophic meltdown, an unsuspecting nation has seen how much greedy and power-hungry mice will play when the cat is non-existent. If the government can learn one regulatory lesson from Wall Street, hopefully it's that a government is supposed to govern. When the FCC, FEC and FTC don't protect the rights of the people, a trusting America will be lied to early and often.

VIEWPOINT 6

> *"Conservatives need to defend the First Amendment, because liberals will attack conservative talk radio as part of their master plan."*

Liberal Attempts to Regulate the Media Will Restrict Conservative Speech

Brian Darling

Efforts to regulate conservative media threaten political speech, argues Brian Darling in the following viewpoint. The Democratic administration hopes to supplant the Fairness Doctrine, established by the Federal Communications Commission (FCC) in 1967, with a proposal that would limit conservative points of view, he claims. For example, Darling maintains, the political Left plans to restrict the number of radio stations conservatives can own as part of a plan to silence conservative talk radio. The majority of Americans share conservative values, and efforts to stifle conservative media threaten the expression of these values, he reasons. Darling is a scholar at the Heritage Foundation, a conservative think tank.

Brian Darling, "Conservative Challenges in 11th Congress," *Human Events*, vol. 64, November 10, 2008, p. 15. Copyright 2008 Human Events Inc. Reproduced by permission.

As you read, consider the following questions:

1. In Brian Darling's view, to what did Democratic senator Chuck Schumer equate conservative viewpoints?
2. What kind of leader does the author think Americans need?
3. In the author's opinion, what percentage of Americans consider themselves very or somewhat conservative?

Concerns are growing that President-Elect Barack Obama and newly-empowered congressional Democrats are preparing a battle plan to silence the Right and establish a permanent liberal majority. Will there be a government crackdown on conservative talk radio and free speech in the workplace? And can conservatives find a charismatic leader who will fight for free markets, smaller government, traditional values and a strong national defense?

Regulating Talk Radio

With the new power they amassed on Nov. 4 [2008], some on the Left appear intent on regulating conservative speech. One need look no further than a giddy Election-Day Sen. Chuck Schumer (D-N.Y.), who stated his support for "fair and balanced" talk radio, then equated conservative viewpoints with "pornography." The Fairness Doctrine, created by the Federal Communications Commission (FCC) in 1967, requires broadcasters to air contrasting viewpoints on controversial issues. It was lifted in 1987 by the FCC.

Legislative attempts to eliminate free speech on conservative-leaning talk radio failed in the last Congress [the 110th], therefore talk radio should prepare for death by a thousand regulations. The Obama administration and Congress will try to implement regulations and laws that will fall short of the actual Fairness Doctrine. But they'll still stifle such talk-show hosts as Rush Limbaugh, Bill O'Reilly, Sean Hannity, John Gibson, Laura Ingraham and Glen Beck.

Curbing Dissent

As popular opposition to the reinstitution of the so-called "Fairness Doctrine" mounts, Barack Obama and the Democrat-dominated Congress will end-run critics with legislation that will curb dissent on talk radio. . . .

By demanding radio stations answer to local community watchdog boards to ensure programming is "balanced," "fair," "diverse," "tolerant" and "serving the public interest locally," [conservative author Brad] O'Leary says the rules and legislation being planned will once again make talk radio accountable to politicians, political activists and bureaucrats at the FCC.

World Net Daily,
April 16, 2009. www.wnd.com.

The liberal Center for American Progress and the ironically titled *Free Press* published a report last year [2007] containing a roadmap to silence conservative talk radio. The following legislative and/or regulatory suggestions are proposed as an alternative to the Fairness Doctrine:

- Restore local and national caps on the ownership of commercial radio stations.
- Ensure greater local accountability over radio licensing.
- Require commercial owners who fail to abide by enforceable pubic interest obligations to pay a fee to support public broadcasting.

These recommendations would restrict conservatives from owning too many stations and tax conservatives when they do not provide broadcasting in the "public interest."

Conservatives need to defend the First Amendment, because liberals will attack conservative talk radio as part of their master plan to secure a permanent liberal majority in Washington, D.C. . . .

Filling the Conservative Void

Republicanism is adrift, but the conservative movement and ideas remain strong. Americans need a leader who will fight for them, preserve their freedoms and not give one inch to those who would chip away at our liberties.

Americans are, as even *Newsweek* admitted, "more instinctively conservative" than liberal. Those conservative values aren't hard to identify: protecting the free market; reducing the size and scope of our ever-expanding government; protecting traditional values and the sanctity of human life; and maintaining a strong national defense.

Who will advance those values is an open question. Gov. Sarah Palin's emergence on the national scene energized disaffected conservatives over the past few months. South Carolina's Jim DeMint, the Senate's most conservative member, and Texas Rep. Jeb Hensarling, head of the conservative Republican Study Committee, both could join forces and lead a congressional revolution. Newt Gingrich may engineer another conservative revolution by organizing and leading the conservative movement. Former Massachusetts Gov. Mitt Romney, Louisiana Gov. Bobby Jindal and Gen. David Petraeus are other potential torch-bearers for the conservative cause.

Conservatives should be patient and wait for a good spokesman to emerge, because conservatives hitching to the wrong horse could cause a major split in the conservative movement. An October [2008] poll by the Tarrance Group and Lake Research Partners found that 57 percent of Americans consider themselves very or somewhat conservative.

Conservatism is alive and well outside the Beltway of Washington D.C. We just need a leader to rally around.

Periodical Bibliography

The following articles have been selected to supplement the diverse views presented in this chapter.

Brennan Center for Justice, et al.	"Breaking Free with Fair Elections: A New Declaration of Independence for Congress," March 2007.
Vanessa Cárdenas	"A Quinceañera Election Party," *La Prensa San Diego*, July 18, 2008.
John Fritze	"'Transparency' Fixes Seen in Congress' Future; Watchdog Groups Push Fuller Disclosure," *USA Today*, January 2, 2009.
Nick Gillespie	"The Positives of Negative Campaigning," *Reason*, November 2006.
Steve Gillmor	"The Role of Social Media in Covering the Political Campaigns," *TechCrunch*, August 23, 2008. www.techcrunch.com.
Michael Grunwald	"The Year of Playing Dirtier," *The Washington Post*, October 27, 2006.
Terry Jones	"Do Political Ads Sway Voters?" *St. Louis Journalism Review*, September 2008.
Kenneth Jost	"Judicial Elections," *CQ Researcher*, April 24, 2009.
Gary Kamiya	"The GOP Goes Back to Its Ugly Roots," Salon.com, October 7, 2008. www.salon.com.
Mark Leibovich	"Campaign Shows Glimpses of Partisan Divide," *International Herald Tribune*, October 30, 2008.
Los Angeles Times	"The Ugly Truths About Campaign Strategy," August 19, 2008.
Richard Stengel	"Getting It Straight," *TIME*, September 29, 2008.

CHAPTER 3

How Should Redistricting Be Managed?

Chapter Preface

Analysts representing both political parties generally agree that redistricting can make or break political careers. "It's no secret why everybody fights so hard," claims Republican National Committee (RNC) attorney Mark Braden. "How you draw the lines has a huge impact on who sits in legislative chambers," he maintains. Redistricting experts use detailed census maps and computers to customize a district block by block, hoping to alter districts to gain political advantage. Indeed, sophisticated technology has made gerrymandering—named for the Massachusetts governor, Elbridge Gerry, who approved a salamander-shaped new district in 1812—much easier than in the past. Although politicians from both parties recognize the threat that partisan redistricting poses, they also recognize its power as a political tool. These conflicting political realities frame the redistricting debate. One controversy in this debate is whether the courts should restrict partisan redistricting.

Those who believe that the federal courts should challenge partisan redistricting plans usually believe themselves to have been the victims of such plans—Democrats and Republicans alike. The U.S. Supreme Court has in fact suggested that some redistricting plans might be overturned. In *Davis v. Bandemer* (1986), for example, Justice Byron R. White wrote in the majority opinion that a redistricting plan would indeed be unconstitutional if it caused "continued frustration of the will of a majority of the voters or effective denial to a minority of voters of a fair chance to influence the political process." Some commentators claim, however, that this standard is very difficult to meet. Indeed, in the same case, the Court refused to overturn the Indiana congressional redistricting plan that was the issue in the case. Critics claim that the U.S. Supreme Court should create a new standard. Pennsylvania Democrats asked the Court to do just that in the 2004 Pennsylvania redistricting case *Vieth v. Jubelirer*. A redistricting plan would be unconstitutional, they maintain, if "the rival party's candidates could be consigned to fewer than half the seats even if its candidates consistently won a majority of votes statewide." The Court has yet to set such a standard, however, or explain what might or might not justify redistricting plans.

Other analysts argue that judicial intervention in the redistricting process puts the integrity of the judiciary at risk. According to law professor Nathaniel Persily, asking federal courts to rule on redistricting plans puts courts "in this incredible position of having to decide . . . which representatives live and die." Moreover, like-minded observers explain, redistricting disputes that create political lines are much different from those that create racial lines, which are clearly unconstitutional. Political voting patterns change over time. Indeed, "the political system does recover," claims political science professor Mark Rush. People change their votes, incumbents retire, and new candidates come forward. "Elections go back and forth. The system works," reasons Rush. In fact, he asserts, the threat posed by partisan redistricting is exaggerated. A few years after the Court in *Bandemer* refused to overturn the Republican-crafted redistricting plan in Indiana, the Democrats regained the majority of congressional seats. "Any extreme attempts at partisan redistricting are self-correcting," claims Republican party attorney John Krill. Efforts to set standards should be left to Congress, these analysts assert.

The fight over redistricting has a long history in the United States, and the debate over the role the judiciary should play in these disputes remains hotly contested. The authors in the following chapter explore similar disputes in the controversy over how redistricting should be managed.

VIEWPOINT 1

> *"Redistricting reform is no panacea, but it is a start."*

Redistricting Reforms Are Necessary

Thomas E. Mann

Redistricting reform will reduce gerrymandering, claims Thomas E. Mann in the following viewpoint. Gerrymandering, the changing of electoral districts to gain political advantage, reduces competition and increases polarization, he asserts. For example, Mann maintains, in 2004 the number of competitive U.S. House seats fell to 6 percent, an all-time low. To reinvigorate the electoral process, he argues, states have several reform options: prohibit mid-decade redistricting, encourage court decisions that overturn unconstitutional gerrymandering plans, or establish nonpartisan redistricting commissions. Mann, a senior fellow at the Brookings Institution, is co-author of several books on political campaigns.

As you read, consider the following questions:

1. According to Thomas E. Mann, in what way is redistricting a deeply political process?

Thomas E. Mann, "Redistricting Reform," *The National Voter*, June 2005, p. 4. Reproduced by permission of the League of Women Voters of the United States, publisher and rights owner.

2. What state has become a prototype for current redistricting reformers, in the author's opinion?
3. In the author's view, who can be expected to oppose redistricting reform efforts?

America is an outlier in the world of democracies when it comes to the structure and conduct of elections. Presidents are elected not by direct popular vote but by 538 members of the Electoral College. Votes in federal elections are cast and counted in a highly decentralized and variable fashion, with no uniform ballots and few national standards. Responsibility for overseeing the implementation of election law typically resides with partisan officials, many with public stakes in the election outcome. And authority for redrawing legislative district boundaries after each decennial census—in the U.S. House of Representatives and in state legislatures—is lodged with political bodies in most of the fifty states.

The latter has long been a prominent and much-criticized feature of American politics. Redistricting is a deeply political process, with incumbents actively seeking to minimize the risk to themselves (via bipartisan gerrymanders) or to gain additional seats for their party (via partisan gerrymanders). But several recent developments have lent a new urgency to this issue and precipitated the most serious effort to reform redistricting processes in many years.

A Decline in Competitive Seats

One recent development is the sharp decline in the number of competitive seats in the House and in most state legislatures. While during the last quarter century the average number of marginal House seats, i.e., those decided within the range of 55 to 45 percent, has been a historically low 58 (13 percent of all seats), the number plummeted after the most recent round of redistricting, reaching 27—6 percent of seats in 2004. Only four House incumbents were defeated by challengers in the

2002 general election, the smallest number in American history. Two years later only seven incumbents were defeated. Less than 50 of the 435 seats were seriously contested in 2002, many fewer than the number of targets in 1972, 1982 and 1992, the first elections after the previous rounds of redistricting. The number of House seats with a real contest shrank to three dozen in 2004.

The same pattern is evident in state legislative races. A prime illustration of this phenomenon is to be found in the largest state, California, where every incumbent seeking reelection won and not a single seat changed party hands in the 2004 congressional and state legislative elections.

Ideological Polarization

In addition to the decline in competition, American politics today is characterized by a growing ideological polarization between the two major political parties. A healthy degree of party unity among Democrats and Republicans has deteriorated into bitter partisan warfare. With the number of moderates in legislative bodies declining, the possibilities of bipartisan negotiation and compromise diminish. Many observers and participants believe redistricting fuels this polarization, by creating safe seats in which incumbents have strong incentives to reflect the views of their party's most extreme supporters—i.e., those active in primary elections—and little reason to reach out to swing voters.

The Role of National Party Leaders

A third development behind the surge of interest in redistricting reform is the more aggressive actions by national party leaders to orchestrate partisan gerrymanders in the states. With the parties at virtual parity and the ideological gulf between them never greater, the stakes of majority control of Congress are extremely high. Norms that once constrained the behavior of party leaders have collapsed.

House Majority Leader Tom DeLay's infamous but successful mid-decade partisan gerrymander in Texas (which cost the Democrats six seats, twice the national gain realized by the Republicans in 2004) has set off a potential redistricting arms race. While the Colorado Republican effort to adopt a second post-2000 redistricting plan was nixed by the state Supreme Court, the party seems to have succeeded in Georgia, if newly drawn maps are pre-cleared by the Justice Department and upheld by the courts. Democrats are considering retaliatory actions in a number of states newly under their political control, including New Mexico, Illinois and Louisiana.

Redistricting Reform

Redistricting reform cannot by itself reverse these trends toward declining electoral competition, increasing ideological polarization between the parties, and smash-mouth partisan manipulation of the electoral rules of the game.

The country is evenly divided between the two parties. Most voters have sorted themselves into a party by their ideological views, and their decisions on where to reside have promoted a geographical segregation of like-minded citizens—conservatives to the exurbs, liberals to cities. Furthermore, partisan attachments powerfully shape political perceptions, beliefs and values, and incumbents enjoy advantages well beyond the way in which their districts are configured. All of these forces will continue to shape our politics no matter what initiatives are taken to improve the process. Redistricting reform is no panacea, but it is a start.

Most states redraw congressional district boundaries through the normal legislative process, constrained by standards set by Congress, the courts, and state constitutions and statutes. Congress requires states to draw single-member districts. The courts insist that all districts within states be of equal population and that minority votes not be diluted. Most states have put redistricting standards in their constitutions or statutes: contiguity, compactness, adherence to political and geographical boundaries, and respect for communities of interest are the most common. However, these state standards suffer from ambiguity, conflict with other standards, and the absence of effective enforcement mechanisms. They have not been a serious constraint on the politicians drawing the maps.

Three Options for Reform

Those seeking to reduce the partisan and incumbent manipulation of the redistricting process have three broad options.

The first is to persuade Congress to adopt additional standards for redistricting by the states. The most prominent proposal would prohibit more than a single round of congressional redistricting after the decennial apportionment. As long as Rep. Tom Delay, the chief architect of the Texas redistricting plan, remains majority leader, this idea is likely to go nowhere. The interesting question is how a Democratic majority in Congress might react to it.

A second option for reformers is to convince the courts to find gerrymandered plans unconstitutional. In *Davis v. Bandemer* (1986) the Supreme Court ruled that partisan gerrymandering is justiciable under the Equal Protection Clause. However, by setting a high threshold for successful challengers ("evidence of continued frustration of the will of a majority of the voters or effective denial to a minority of voters of a fair chance to influence the political process"), the Court rendered this standard ineffectual. Only one successful partisan gerrymandering claim—in a judicial election—has been litigated under the *Bandemer* ruling.

Last year [2004] the Court returned to this question by considering a case brought by Pennsylvania Democrats. Its decision in *Vieth v. Jubelirer* (2004) appears to have maintained the status quo. While all nine justices acknowledged that partisan gerrymandering could be unconstitutional, in rejecting the challenge the majority despaired of finding workable standards for determining when it was. Litigation challenging the Texas mid-decade redistricting plan continues, but the federal courts do not appear a promising venue for reform. Prospects for countering anti-competitive bipartisan plans are even bleaker. In past decisions, the Court has explicitly sanctioned the protection of incumbency as a legitimate redistricting objective.

The third and clearly most promising avenue of reform is to change the process by which states draw legislative maps. Often facing entrenched opposition in state legislatures, reformers are increasingly turning to the initiative process to establish independent, nonpartisan redistricting commissions.

Six states—Arizona, Hawaii, Idaho, Montana, New Jersey and Washington—already invest commissions with a first and final authority for congressional redistricting. Another, Indiana, uses a commission as a backup if the normal legislative process fails to produce a plan. Two other states, Maine and Connecticut, use commissions in an advisory capacity: Their plans must be approved by the legislature before taking effect. One state, Iowa, delegates authority for drafting redistricting plans to a nonpartisan legislative support staff agency, which operates under a "veil of ignorance" with respect to the addresses of incumbents, partisan affiliation of voters and previous election results. However, the Iowa legislature retains the authority to put its own mark on the ultimate plan.

A Model for Reform

Arizona has become a prototype for current reformers. The state's independent redistricting commission was established by popular initiative in 2000. Four members (two from each party) are appointed by state legislative leaders from a pool approved by a judicial appointments panel. The four appointees then select a fifth member (drawn from a comparable pool but not affiliated with either party) to serve as chair. Commission maps are approved by majority vote and are not

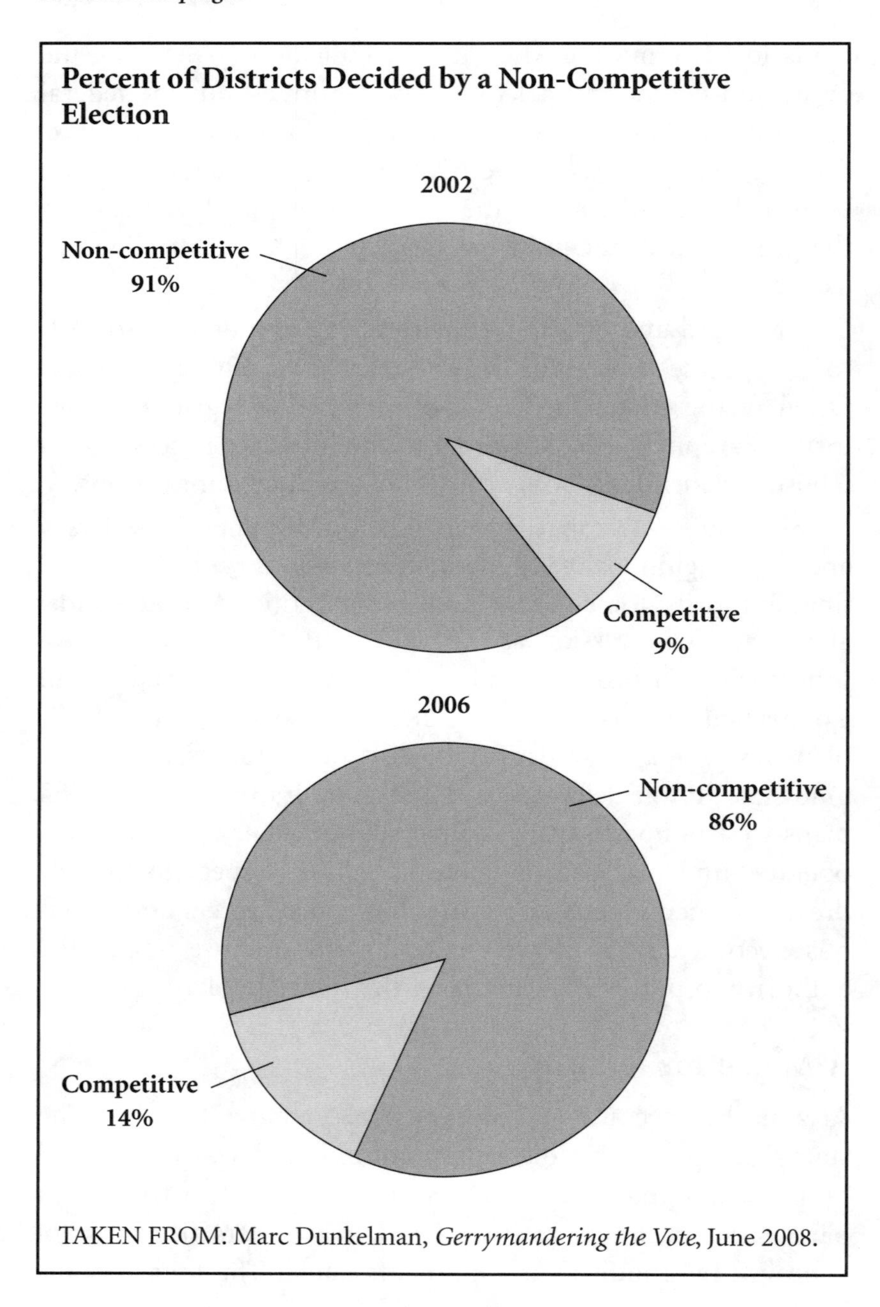

TAKEN FROM: Marc Dunkelman, *Gerrymandering the Vote*, June 2008.

subject to review by the legislature or veto by the governor. The commission is given explicit standards and procedures to follow in drawing redistricting plans. Importantly, these include favoring competitive districts and not identifying or considering the place of residence of incumbents or candidates.

Efforts to adopt some variation of the Arizona system are underway in a number of states. California governor Arnold Schwarzenegger has proposed investing redistricting authority in a panel of retired judges. If he fails to reach agreement with the Democratic legislature, the governor will lead an effort to place an initiative on the ballot later this year.

A number of organizations, including the Center for Governmental Studies [CGS], Demos and Common Cause, have issued guidelines for how redistricting commissions should be structured, members selected, and operating standards and procedures established. The devil is often in the details. Critics have expressed concerns with draft California initiative language, on grounds that it authorizes a second, mid-decade redistricting plan and that its provisions to ensure partisan fairness and competitiveness may be inadequate.

In other states, nonprofit organizations and unions are taking the lead to draft and qualify initiatives for state ballots. The League of Women Voters at the state level has been active, too. Twenty-four states allow citizen initiatives on their ballots, and efforts are underway in Colorado, Florida, Massachusetts and Ohio to adopt redistricting commissions. In states without a provision for popular initiative, reformers must navigate the normal state legislative process to alter the redistricting process.

Incumbent officeholders and party leaders can be expected to oppose these efforts, since they are wary of changes that might diminish their individual reelection prospects or remove from their arsenal a weapon that might help them achieve or maintain majority control. But these self-interested calculations could lead to other preferences, depending on the particular political circumstances in each individual state. In some states, one party or the other may well conclude that they would fare better with a redistricting commission than with the status quo.

Conditions have improved for a major reconsideration of the manner in which legislative boundaries are redrawn. Success depends very much on the level of sustained interest and engagement by citizens across the country.

Viewpoint 2

"Parties will continue to fight fervently in state legislatures to make plans that help their cause or prevent the other from gaining too much of an advantage."

Redistricting Reforms Are Unlikely

Dan Seligson

The political climate in the United States along with recent decisions of the U.S. Supreme Court make redistricting reforms highly unlikely in the near future, asserts Dan Seligson in the following viewpoint. While lawsuits objecting redistricting efforts will continue, Seligson observes that the Court seems strongly divided, with a narrow majority approving a controversial Texas gerrymander (the changing of electoral districts to gain political advantage). While nearly half of the states plan redistricting reform legislation, the battles will be fierce, as political parties will always fight for plans that give their party the advantage, he concludes. Seligson is an election administration expert. He writes, edits, and is project manager for electionline.org, a project of the Pew Center on the States that serves as a nonpartisan source for election reform news and analysis.

As you read, consider the following questions:

1. In Dan Seligson's view, why is the 2003 mid-decade Texas redistricting plan so memorable?
2. According to the author, how many states have commission systems?
3. Which state's plan do most experts think is fair to both sides, in the author's opinion?

The typically once-a-decade process of carving up the nation into districts for state and federal offices is a confounding, bitter and litigious process. But with pain comes gains: namely, a more secure hold on power for years to come.

With the presidential primary season already underway (and the 2006 election just past) it wouldn't seem to be the most obvious time for political parties and pundits to contemplate the next session of remapping. But think again.

Is It Time for Remapping?

Legislation in several state houses could shift responsibility for who draws new districts. The Voting Rights Act, requiring some states to get federal approval for redistricting plans, was just reauthorized. A recent Supreme Court decision [*League of United Latin American Citizens v. Perry*, June 2006] on a Texas redistricting plan essentially gave the green light for continued gerrymandering, steering clear of voiding a map drawn up by Texas Republicans to bolster their power.

And then there are the Democrats, who assumed control of Congress along with a multitude of governorships and state legislature seats. They may want to wield their new power by reversing Republicans' redistricting fortunes from 2000–2001. And they may want to start putting their stamp on the electoral map well before the next U.S. Census (in 2010), which typically precedes redistricting.

Copyright 2002 by Jeff Parker, Florida Today and CagleCartoons.com.

It would seem the time is ripe for a mid-decade political remap. But, as experts note, things are not always what they seem.

Most experts predict the next round of redistricting will look largely like those before it, except perhaps with Democrats more firmly in control in many states. Another Texas debacle is unlikely. In political economics, the resources that would be required to redistrict—from political capital to time spent on remapping rather than other priorities—will likely far outstrip potential gains.

Not Another Texas

Partisan shifts across the country suggest the next round of redistricting might come before 2010. But a closer look reveals that midterm redistricting is fairly unlikely.

States could decide to undertake mid-decade redistricting, as happened in Texas in 2003. That year, a plan crafted by former House majority leader Tom DeLay, R-Texas, stacked the odds for a GOP [Grand Old Party, the nickname for the Republican Party] power boost in Congress. Many recall the midnight flight and ensuing partisan standoff when Democratic lawmakers hopped the border to Oklahoma in order to make it impossible for the Republicans to hold a vote on the plan. And, of course, the efforts of law enforcement, ordered by DeLay, to track down the Dems and bring them back to Austin.

Three years later, the Supreme Court struck down one of those new districts, the 23rd, held by Rep. Henry Bonilla, R-Texas, because it diluted partisan voting power by carving up Latino neighborhoods, which tend to vote Democrat. But by a 5–4 margin, the Court upheld the rest of the 2003 plan, clearing the way for a legislature to rewrite a previously drawn legislative map for no other reason than partisan advantage.

Bolstered by gains in Congress and statehouses, is it payback time?

Doubtful, said Tim Storey, a redistricting expert and election analyst for the Denver-based National Conference of State Legislatures [NCSL].

"The idea that we will see a new round of mid-decade redistricting is misleading," he said. "Once you boil it down, you see it's highly unlikely that states would plug back into [redistricting]."

Storey pointed to a number of reasons why state partisans wouldn't be able to alter maps drawn after the 2000 census.

First, a party must have unified control in the legislature and the governorship. Right now, only 25 states have such conditions in place. Subtract the states that by law have bipartisan or nonpartisan commissions that draw maps, and you're left with 21. Of those, at least a third have constitutional entanglements that wouldn't make redistricting feasible.

Then, of course, there are the small states (including Alaska, Delaware, Montana, both Dakotas, Vermont and

Wyoming) that only have one U.S. House district, simplifying the process considerably by eliminating it.

Take the three states still standing—Ohio, Florida and Texas—and you might not have the political will to undertake a process in which there might not be an opportunity to make substantial gains in the legislature.

And then, there is only one Texas.

Mark Braden, an attorney who has represented the GOP in redistricting cases, said Texas had "an incredible Democratic gerrymander" in 2000 as well as DeLay, a firebrand who didn't earn the nickname "The Hammer" for his carpentry skills.

"Absent one or the other, you wouldn't have had [mid-decade redistricting] in Texas," Braden said.

In short, the costs of redistricting could be just too high to justify any modest political gains. But that's not to say the process will be exactly the same as in previous years. From changes in redistricting commissions to new court rulings, there's definitely room for change.

Looking at Legislative Action

State lawmakers are considering bills that would alter what is typically a system of winner-map-all—whereby the party in power draws up a map for an up or down vote—to one that would create bipartisan or nonpartisan redistricting commissions.

Legislation to alter the redistricting process is pending in at least 25 states. States that approve a commission system would join the dozen states that currently have similar panels. According to NCSL data, commissions in 12 states (including Arizona, Colorado, Missouri, New Jersey, Ohio and Pennsylvania) already have "primary responsibility" for creating redistricting plans.

Ideally, experts say, a commission helps to streamline the convoluted and contentious partisan process in which one party draws the map, the other objects and a court intervenes.

But rules that govern the partisan makeup of some commissions can give one party a clear advantage.

Michael McDonald, a political science professor at George Mason University, said Ohio's rules, coupled with Democratic control of top statewide offices, could trigger a redistricting war.

"In Ohio, Democrats control two of three statewide offices, they were just elected in the last election and everyone is predicting the incumbents will win," McDonald said. "Most likely, you'll have a Democratic governor, secretary of state, and Democratic control of the state legislature by 2013. Then you could have the exact same situation as Texas."

And a stacked commission in which one party runs roughshod over another is just one problem. Another more basic concern is that even commission plans drawn with the best bipartisan intentions also fail.

The Next Round of Redistricting

All of which leads to the inevitable question of what shape the next round of redistricting might take.

Certainly there could be some wrinkles, McDonald says, but the process will not be all that changed from previous years. If a Democrat retakes the White House, the U.S. Department of Justice will have to make difficult choices when deciding whether to authorize redistricting plans in the states that fall under Section 5 of the 1964 Voting Rights Act: Alabama, Arizona, Georgia, Louisiana, Mississippi, South Carolina, Texas and Virginia. (These states, along with some jurisdictions in other states, had a history of discrimination against minority-group voters, along with low turnout among those groups.)

"If the Democrats do control the Department of Justice, they probably will not be eager to pack minority districts," he said. "In the past two rounds, we've seen the department really want to pack in minority voters. And Democrats want to shave down margins so they can spread black voters into other districts and boost Democratic chances."

The immigration issue could factor in as well. While Hispanic voters are not as reliably Democratic as black voters, the recent wave of anti-immigration sentiment has been largely viewed as anti-Hispanic. And the backlash will almost certainly be felt at the polls.

There will also likely be more lawsuits, even if there are more states with bipartisan commissions.

"There is going to be a blizzard of lawsuits, frankly, because the law has become more confusing than before," Braden said. "The partisan gerrymandering issue has been a difficult one for the Supreme Court for a long time, and it's fractured on it. Do commissions make it easier? They make it easier for lawyers to litigate. Arizona has a commission, and their [2001 redistricting plan] is still in litigation."

Sam Hirsch, an attorney at Jenner & Block who has represented the Democratic Party on redistricting issues, said one trend this round could be the increasing importance of state laws and state courts.

After the 2000 election, there was a renewed emphasis on maintaining jurisdictional borders in the redistricting process. A number of challenges to state plans, he said, were based on redistricting maps not complying with county lines. That should continue, if not increase, in 2010.

No Improvements Are Likely

So what can we expect? More of the same: a redistricting process that is as cumbersome and complicated as it is acrimonious.

Parties will continue to fight fervently in state legislatures to make plans that help their cause or prevent the other from gaining too much of an advantage. Commissions will perhaps make the process easier in some states; most experts think New Jersey's plan is fair to both sides, competitive in its political districts and respectful of local boundaries. But an improved process in 2010 might be too much to expect.

"The fact that we have so many court-drawn districts shows that we have something wrong with the system," Hirsch said. "Out of the 50 states, somewhere in the 40s end up having their plans in court. In 2004 and 2002, 16 percent of all congressional districts were decided by federal and state courts. Is there something wrong with that? Absolutely."

Viewpoint 3

> *"A well-designed redistricting commission should better represent the interests of the public than legislators, who may allow potential political gain to dictate their actions."*

Independent Commissions Can Reduce Political Redistricting

Scott M. Lesowitz

Independent redistricting commissions can reduce partisan gerrymandering, or redistricting for political gain, argues Scott M. Lesowitz in the following viewpoint. When legislators determine how districts are created, the potential for abuse increases because legislators who feel secure in their reelection may be less accountable to their constituents, he maintains. Commissioners selected by a unanimous vote of representatives from both parties could significantly reduce redistricting bias, Lesowitz asserts. Nevertheless, he claims, the redistricting process should not be completely apolitical, as the goal is to create districts that represent the needs of its voters. Lesowitz works for the U.S. Attorney's Office in San Diego, California.

Scott M. Lesowitz, "Independent Redistricting Commissions," *Harvard Journal on Legislation*, vol. 43, 2006, p. 535.

As you read, consider the following questions:

1. According to Scott M. Lesowitz, what factors weighed against Proposition 77 and State Issue 4?
2. What does the author say is a serious problem for creators of commissions aimed specifically at preventing gerrymandering?
3. In the author's view, how can independent commissions help minorities?

In 2001, a divided Texas legislature deadlocked over the drawing of congressional districts. In response, a panel of federal judges instituted a compromise redistricting plan. In the following election, using the congressional districts drawn by these judges, Texas voters elected seventeen Democrats and fifteen Republicans to the United States House of Representatives. At the state level, Republicans fared better, winning control of both houses of the Texas legislature. Then, in 2003, those Texas legislature Republicans broke with tradition and began a campaign to perform a second round of redistricting based on the 2000 census data.

A struggle ensued between Texas Democrats and Republicans, but the new redistricting plan eventually passed. The results of the 2004 election using the new redistricting plan were drastically different from the results of the 2002 election: whereas Texans elected seventeen Democrats and fifteen Republicans in 2002 to the U.S. House of Representatives, in 2004 they elected eleven Democrats and twenty-one Republicans. While it is debatable just how egregious the Republican-led redistricting plan was, this election does demonstrate the potential power of a legislature to adjust political outcomes through the redistricting process—a practice that has been employed by Democrats and Republicans alike.

Efforts to Avoid Partisan Gerrymandering

Shortly after these events in Texas, on June 13, 2005, California governor Arnold Schwarzenegger called a special election in which Californians would vote on four propositions designed to address California's budgetary woes and reform the political process in the state. One of the four measures, Proposition 77, called for the creation of an independent commission, composed of three retired judges, to replace the state legislature as the chief body in charge of performing redistricting in California. Californians rejected Proposition 77 by a fairly sizeable margin. On the same day, Ohio voters also decisively defeated State Issue 4, a ballot measure that would have created an independent redistricting commission there.

However, the defeat of Proposition 77 and State Issue 4 does not necessarily mean that the public does not support redistricting reform. For instance, Arizona voters passed an initiative creating an independent redistricting commission in 2000. Also, there were numerous factors weighing against the two doomed ballot propositions. For instance, Proposition 77's fate was likely tied to the unpopularity of its chief supporter, Governor Schwarzenegger; public disapproval of the special election and its expense in general; efforts by both major political parties against the measure; and historic skepticism toward redistricting commissions in California. State Issue 4 was likely harmed by perceptions that it was a ploy by Democrats to increase their political power and that it used a confusing formula to perform redistricting, producing sample redistricting plans that "looked like strands of spaghetti thrown against a wall." Further, while California voters rejected Proposition 77, polls indicated that a majority of likely California voters supported making some sort of change in the redistricting process. In addition, numerous other states are considering adopting independent commissions to per-

Gerrymandering by the Numbers

23	Number of House races, out of 435, decided by less than 10 percent in 2004.
98	Percentage of House incumbents to win re-election in 2004.
6	Number of states that have attempted to conduct mid-decade "re-redistricting" since 2000.

TAKEN FROM: Campaign Legal Center, *Redistricting Problems and Solutions*, 2007.

form redistricting in the future. The lessons that the stories of Proposition 77 and State Issue 4 provide are pertinent to future redistricting reform efforts. . . .

The Complex Issues of Competition and Partisan Representation

One of the frequent arguments for independent redistricting commissions is that they are needed to ensure competitive races. In 2002, less than ten percent of congressional elections were decided by fewer than ten percentage points, and only four congressional incumbents lost general election races for reelection. The concern is that if redistricting is left to the state legislature and the governor, aided by advanced modern technology, they will draw districts in a way to ensure easy re-election for incumbents or to further partisan advantage. The lack of competition may lead to unaccountable legislators who have little to fear from the electoral process. Similarly, shifts in voter alignment may not be reflected adequately in electoral outcomes. Furthermore, the creation of districts heavily favoring one political persuasion may lead to the victory of ideologically extreme candidates, who do not feel compelled to appeal to the politically moderate. The evidence suggests that gerrymandering is one cause of lack of competition, though the causal relationship can be exaggerated.

However, a serious problem for creators of independent redistricting commissions aimed at preventing gerrymandering is that there is no such thing as purely neutral redistricting criteria. Even seemingly apolitical criteria may lead to low levels of competitiveness and may also systematically hinder the political fortunes of one of the major political parties. Redistricting commissions should utilize election and partisan data to adjust redistricting plans so that they are not unduly biased against one of the major political parties and to ensure adequate levels of competition. . . .

Rating the Anti-Bias Mechanisms

One of the primary reasons to employ an independent commission to perform redistricting is to prevent officials from drawing district lines in a manner designed to achieve political gain. When creating a redistricting system, it is important that the system ensure the highest level of impartiality.

The regimes envisioned by Proposition 77 and State Issue 4 would have gone to great lengths to ensure that redistricting commission members would not have had conflicts of interests with either the government or a political party. State Issue 4 would have placed restrictions on political activity and business with political actors after service on the commission. Such restrictive policies seem crucial to ensuring that members of redistricting commissions will be as nonpartisan as possible and not tempted by the possibility of future political or financial gain. Even if a commission is balanced in partisanship, if the commission members are too politically connected, they may sponsor a plan that helps to ensure electoral victory for incumbents from both parties; both parties would be interested in ensuring easy reelection for their incumbents.

State Issue 4 also would have attempted to limit bias by giving the members of the redistricting commission very little personal leeway in the redistricting process. The measure enumerated very specific criteria to be followed. In fact, most of the process could have been performed by a computer. However, while such a system can help to prevent abuses, it also creates inflexibility and inhibits honest commissioners from better implementing comments from the public and from avoiding previously unanticipated problems.

Establishing Safeguards

Proposition 77 also would have employed commission member selection mechanisms that might have lessened the chance of bias and partisanship. One mechanism employed by Proposition 77 was that the four state legislators involved in the selection process would have evenly represented the minority and majority parties. Also, each partisan politician could only have nominated candidates for the commission who did not belong to the same political party as he did. Presumably, a politician would not pick someone from the other party who is known as a partisan ideologue or who is likely to be unfair. A commission of neutral members is less likely to be biased and more likely to compromise than an evenly divided commission of partisans.

Another safeguard was that each major political party would have to have been represented on the commission and a unanimous vote would have been required for ratification of a redistricting plan. Thus, a member of each major party would have to have supported the plan, preventing supporters of one political party from taking over the process, though this also could have led to deadlocks. Additionally, the Judicial

Council would have picked the twenty-four people from which the four legislators would have chosen. While judges are not always apolitical, presumably a judicial body would be less political in its selections than a legislative body. Also, allowing each of the four legislators involved in the selection process to strike a nominee from consideration would have helped to ferret out problematic candidates.

One peculiar provision of Proposition 77's selection process was that the three members of the redistricting commission would have been chosen at random from the remaining pool of nominees after each legislator was afforded an opportunity to strike a nominee. Problematic candidates could have survived the lottery. Also, immensely qualified and fair candidates, who would enjoy universal approval, could have been removed by the lottery. A better mechanism to achieve neutrality would have been to have the legislators initially nominate eleven candidates and then require each legislator to strike two candidates.

Democratic Accountability

Drawing legislative districts carries significant political ramifications that affect the average citizen. One common critique of creating independent redistricting commissions is that it puts redistricting in the hands of unelected officials who have little or no accountability to the voters. A related argument is that the independent redistricting commissions will be unrepresentative of the diverse population of a state.

One problem with the arguments that independent redistricting commissions are too unaccountable is that they assume elected politicians are more accountable. In fact, elected politicians may calculate that the political gains from gerrymandering are potentially so great that they outweigh any potential backlash from voters.

Also, even if the redistricting commissions are less responsive to some of the concerns of voters, the political system overall may become more accountable. If an independent redistricting commission is well-designed, the plan it produces should make elections more competitive. Since more competitive elections should make politicians more accountable generally, this increased responsiveness may outweigh any loss of accountability in the redistricting process. . . .

Avoiding Design Flaws

There has long been concern about allowing legislators to draw the districts in which they face reelection. There is potential for legislators to collude to draw safe districts that incumbents can win easily. Also, there is the possibility that one political party will control the state legislature and the governorship and will use their power to gerrymander the state's districts to enhance their future electoral prospects at the expense of their opponents and the democratic process.

Designers of redistricting commissions need to be aware of the potential ramifications of their system and of its possible flaws. Even if the only goal of a commission system is to remove the possibility of the worst abuses of gerrymandering, designers must be careful not to introduce unintended consequences. Using seemingly apolitical redistricting criteria may unfairly harm the political prospects of one political party and result in low levels of competition. Partisan voting data and preferences would have to be utilized to adjust district lines to achieve minimum levels of competition and results that are not unduly biased against one political party.

This article posits that redistricting commissions can be created without significant problems with political bias. An ideal system should not just rely on bipartisanship to achieve neutrality. A collection of neutral people should be better at both working together and achieving fairness than a politically balanced group of ideologues. Efforts to keep politically connected people off of the commission, to curtail potential abuse of discretion, and to limit dealings with political figures after service on the panel will minimize the costs of entrusting commissions with political data.

While there are legitimate concerns about the democratic accountability of independent redistricting commissions, on balance a well-designed redistricting commission should better represent the interests of the public than legislators, who may allow potential political gain to dictate their actions. Also, federal law protects minorities in the redistricting process, and the new statute or amendment creating the redistricting commission can provide extra guarantees to minorities if federal law is deemed inadequate. The redistricting commission should be required to take public input, as was the case in both Proposition 77 and State Issue 4, and the redistricting commission should be given enough flexibility to take this input into account.

On the whole, the complex issues that are raised by creating a redistricting commission may make the endeavor impracticable, especially since the negative effects of political gerrymandering can be exaggerated. However, if a commission is crafted with enough thought, care, help from statisticians, and input from the public about its views on what a fair redistricting system would achieve, a fairer redistricting commission system should result.

Viewpoint 4

"Reformers across the country should recognize that publicly financed elections and independent redistricting commissions are valuable but insufficient reforms."

Independent Commissions Will Not Reduce Political Redistricting

Steven Hill

While creating independent redistricting commissions to reduce partisan gerrymandering (or redistricting for political gain) is admirable, the results have been disappointing, claims Steven Hill in the following viewpoint. Arizona, the leader in state election reform, has, in fact, had some of the least competitive elections, he asserts. Competitive elections are what many expect to be the result of successful electoral reform. In 2004, Iowa, the state with what some claim is the ideal independent commission, reelected all congressional incumbents, countering claims that such commissions increase competition. Political activist Hill is author of Fixing Elections: The Failure of America's Winner Take All Politics.

Steven Hill, "Keep on Reforming," Salon.com, June 13, 2005. This article first appeared in Salon.com at http://www.salon.com. An online version remains in the Salon archives. Reprinted with permission.

As you read, consider the following questions:

1. What does Steven Hill say accompanied electoral reforms in the few states that enacted them?
2. How did political races change in Washington State between the 1990s and 2004, in the author's view?
3. What state does the author cite as a case of "demography is destiny"?

Politics involves the art of achieving the possible. Rarely do you get what you want, so you take what you can get. But when it comes to electoral reform, reformers run the risk of overpromising in trying to gain attention for their particular issue—and can end up underdelivering, increasing voters' cynicism.

Two of the most talked-about electoral reforms in the past decade have been the public financing of election campaigns and the use of independent commissions to redraw legislative district lines. While reformers have had limited success passing those two reforms—to date [in 2005], only a handful of states use either public financing or independent commissions, and even fewer use both—when enacted, the reforms have been accompanied by great fanfare and hope.

Yet the impact of the two reforms has been disappointing, and it may be time to extend our efforts at reform to the primary culprit in our broken democracy: our winner-take-all elections.

Arizona's Disappointing Reforms

Arizona, for example, has led the nation in electoral reforms, but so far has had limited results. The Grand Canyon State passed voter initiatives in 1998 and 2000 that enacted both full public financing for state elections and an independent redistricting commission. Yet recently when I gave a speech at the annual convention of the Arizona League of Women Voters, which had spearheaded the state's reform efforts, I was surprised to hear the frustration voiced by many league members and other Arizona reformers. The post-reform electoral results have neither fulfilled their expectations nor matched the campaign hype that sold the reforms to voters.

Indeed, Arizona now has some of the least competitive races in the nation, which is not what one would expect from a state with both a redistricting commission and public financing. All eight congressional incumbents won reelection last year by landslide margins, an average of 34 percent. In the state Senate, none of the 30 seats were competitive, and more than half of the seats were uncontested by one of the two major parties. In the state House, half the races were uncontested by a major party and only five of 60 races were competitive. And 97 percent of the incumbents won reelection, whether they had publicly financed or privately financed races.

To be sure, there have been positive developments in Arizona too, such as an increase in the number of candidates running in primaries and for statewide executive offices, fostering more political debate. And 10 of 11 state officeholders accepted public financing, including Democratic Gov. Janet Napolitano. On the other hand, the legislature has turned increasingly right-wing, and there has been no noticeable impact on legislative policy.

So, after all their hard work, it's not surprising that Arizona reformers expressed frustration. And Arizona is not alone in seeing disappointing results.

Reforms in Other States

Iowa has been held up as the poster child for the effectiveness of redistricting commissions, yet in 2004 all congressional incumbents easily won reelection, and the average margin of victory was a landslide of 18 percent. In the state legislature, 61 percent of seats in the House were won by landslide margins, 85 percent by noncompetitive margins of 10 points or more. Only four seats out of 100 were won by less than a five-point margin, and the average margin of victory was a whopping 47 percent.

In Washington state, whose bipartisan redistricting commission produced some of the most competitive races of the 1990s, only one of nine congressional races was close in 2004; the average margin of victory was 28 percent.

In the state legislature, huge numbers of races went uncontested. Republicans dominate almost every legislative district east of the Cascade Mountains and Democrats win almost every district in King County, the most populous, with Seattle as its seat. Other states with a redistricting commission have had similarly disappointing results.

Maine does not use an independent redistricting commission, but it does have public financing for state elections. Results have been somewhat better than in other states but are nothing to crow about.

On the positive side, the number of contested primaries rose to 39 in 2004, up from 25 in 2000, fostering more political debate. And in the November [2004] election only two races were uncontested by a major party in the state Senate, and seven in the House. But Maine remains dogged by noncompetitive elections: In 2004 the average victory margin for 35 state Senate races and 151 state House races was a landslide of 20 points. Only four races in the Senate were highly competitive (won by less than five points), while 31 in the House were, but 62 House races were won by landslide margins.

Winner-Take-All Electoral Systems

With such disappointing results in state after state, the temptation might arise to abandon these reforms as ineffective. That would be a mistake. It's not that they aren't good reforms; it's just that they're more limited in their impact than most people realize—or than reformers, caught up in their zeal, are willing to admit.

Here's what's going on in these and other states that makes public financing and redistricting commissions less potent: They have reached the limits of what can be accomplished within the confines of their antiquated winner-take-all electoral systems.

Under winner-take-all, a geographically based system, districts elect members of Congress and most state legislators one seat at a time; the candidate with the most votes wins, even if the tally isn't a majority of the total votes cast—and everyone else loses. This system can deny representation to both majorities and minorities, and discourages voter turnout.

We've used this system for a long time (since the 18th century), but over the past 15 years something unusual has been occurring. Regional partisan demographics have been aligning in such a way that certain parts of many states have become solidly Democratic blue or Republican red. The result of this balkanization is that legislative seats that had previously been up for grabs have become one-party fiefdoms. And there's little that either redistricting commissions or publicly financed elections can do to counter that. Demography, it turns out, is destiny.

California is a case in point. In his bid to break the back of special interests and return government to the people, Gov. Arnold Schwarzenegger announced his determination to take redistricting out of the hands of the Democratic-controlled state Legislature. His campaign has created great populist sound bites, but there's just one problem: The plan won't work.

Why Electoral Reforms Aren't Working

In California, liberals and Democrats dominate the coastal areas and cities, while conservatives and Republicans dominate the interior areas. To draw competitive districts, one would have to start districts in downtown San Francisco and extend them in narrow bands, like the spokes of a wheel, eastward

Unanswered Questions

Will minorities who have won hard-fought gains in legislative representation be satisfied with an Independent Redistricting Commission of just a few elites? Could a commission actually create a significant number of competitive districts? Would it drive up campaign costs? What other structural problems in the election system and legislative process need to be examined?

These issues need scrutiny when considering if the people should turn over an important legislative function to an unelected but well-meaning elite.

Gerry Cohen,
"Can We Commission Better Redistricting,"
The News & Observer *(Raleigh, NC),*
November 26, 2006.

across the bay into Contra Costa County (the conservative area). In Los Angeles, one would have to extend the districts eastward into Riverside and San Bernardino counties, with some being little more than narrow east-west bands up and down the state, a design one pundit branded the "coral snakeamander" plan.

Such districts not only would look ridiculous but also would undermine the ability of like-minded voters, especially racial minorities, to elect their representatives and would therefore end up being challenged in court. These daunting demographics will completely thwart Schwarzenegger's attempts to shake up government.

In Arizona, liberals and Democrats are more numerous in the southern part of the state around Tucson, while conservatives and Republicans dominate the rest of the state, including Phoenix. The only way to make winner-take-all districts more competitive would be to draw narrow bands that extended vertically from south to north, like the teeth of a comb.

Partisan demographics and winner-take-all elections also result in the election of fewer moderate legislators and more extremists in places like Arizona. With so many districts locked up as Republican, a right-wing candidate who wins the Republican primary is guaranteed to win the general election. And in a primary with multiple candidates, the right-winger can win with a low percentage of the vote by mobilizing a core of rabid supporters.

In short, California, Arizona and many other states find themselves in a new paradigm in which the problem is not simply who draws the legislative lines, or whether one candidate greatly outspends the other, but partisan balkanization, in which legislators are elected via a checkerboard electoral map of individual districts. These states' winner-take-all electoral system has reached its endgame.

The Way Forward

The way forward is to get rid of the winner-take-all system and adopt the electoral method used in places such as Peoria, Ill.; Amarillo, Texas; Cambridge, Mass.; and dozens of other local jurisdictions. This method employs multiseat districts in a way that greatly increases competition and makes public financing of candidates much more effective.

For example, instead of electing 30 state senators from 30 individual districts, Arizona voters in six larger "super-districts" could elect five senators each. With a Peoria-type electoral method, any candidate who won at least a sixth of the vote would earn one of the district's five seats. These five-seat districts likely would be bipartisan, electing some Republicans in liberal areas and some Democrats in conservative areas, greatly decreasing balkanization. Moderates, independents and occasionally even a third-party candidate would win a fair share of seats. Since all regions of the state would be competitive, voters would have more choice across the political spectrum, regardless of where they live. Not surprisingly, other nations that employ this kind of "proportional representation" system consistently enjoy voter turnout levels twice that of U.S. congressional elections.

Reformers across the country should recognize that publicly financed elections and independent redistricting commissions are valuable but insufficient reforms. If we want to revive American democracy, it is necessary to get rid of our antiquated winner-take-all electoral system.

VIEWPOINT 5

> *"Playing God with geography for political gain dramatically impacts the lives of every voter, but especially Blacks, Hispanics and other groups struggling for power."*

Redistricting Strategies Hurt Minority Voters

Tracie Powell

Modern redistricting strategies make it difficult for minorities to elect people who effectively represent them, claims Tracie Powell in the following viewpoint. Computers make it easy to identify where minorities live and to create districts that neutralize their impact, she asserts. For example, Powell maintains, a member of Congress who represents a large district with mostly rural white constituents cannot effectively represent the district's middle-class blacks, as their concerns are very different. Strengthening the Voting Rights Act, civil rights legislation meant to eliminate electoral racism, may help give voice to minority voters, she argues. Powell is a journalist in Washington, D.C.

Tracie Powell, "Drawn Out of the Game: Some Voters and Scholars Say Redistricting Recalls the Specter of Disenfranchisement," *Diverse Issues in Higher Education*, vol. 23, October 5, 2006, pp. 38–42. www.diverseeducation.com

As you read, consider the following questions:

1. In Tracie Powell's view, what is redistricting all about?
2. How has politics changed since the authorization of the Voting Rights Act, in the author's opinion?
3. According to John N. Friedman and Richard T. Holden, in what states are the most gerrymandered maps found?

The way today's legislators draw political boundary lines reminds Deralyn Davis of the kinds of obstacles that kept Blacks from voting back when her grandmother had to pay $1.75 for the privilege.

The Fort Worth native is a tough, no-nonsense 71-year-old grandmother who stared down bigots and ignored threats while traveling throughout the South to register voters during the late 1960s. But when politicians recently redrew political boundary lines in her state, Davis says they ended any chance she and other minorities had of electing candidates of their choice.

Now she's afraid her past struggles mean nothing.

A Modern Day Poll Tax

"This is the backdoor way to disenfranchise minorities all over again," Davis says. "It's the modern day poll tax."

This November's mid-term elections [2006] could propel Black leaders to the most powerful positions in the U.S. House of Representatives, provided Democrats manage to take control of the chamber. But some political observers say redistricting ploys could play a large role in keeping Democrats out of power for another term.

Redistricting—it's basic to American democracy, but has grown increasingly complex. Complicated or not, playing God with geography for political gain dramatically impacts the lives of every voter, but especially Blacks, Hispanics and other groups struggling for power.

Each year, across the country, hundreds of politicians are chosen for office—long before the first voter casts his or her ballot. Computer technicians, at the behest of politicians, use sophisticated software to draw bizarrely shaped legislative districts that determine who gets elected and, ultimately, what issues get debated.

Redistricting is all about getting and keeping power. Blacks, Hispanics and other minorities say it's tough enough just getting their representatives into office, and they fear that redistricting is making things worse. Many scholars and activists argue that if the party in power continues to be allowed to draw districts that favor their candidates, minority voters will increasingly find themselves drawn out of the game.

Redrawing Political Boundaries

Democrats and Republicans, depending on which party is in control, commonly cram opponents into as few districts as possible, limiting their voting power, or spread them across several districts so that there is no way these voters can impact an election. Insiders call the strategies used to dilute voting strength packing and cracking.

But that's old school.

Legislators now use another method that puts ardent supporters in the same district with a slightly smaller number of ardent opponents. The technique, called matching, effectively neutralizes the opposition, according to a Harvard University study by Drs. John N. Friedman and Richard T. Holden, two economists studying the decline of competitive elections. Their report, released last spring, details the effects of matching and other redistricting strategies. According to the study, the practice of matching is having a significant negative effect on minority representation. National statistics show that more than 90 percent of incumbents return to office, and only five to 10 lose their seat each election cycle. The new "matching strategy" is making it even more likely that politicians can choose their voters instead of the other way around.

"It's quite a novel idea;" says Holden, now at the Massachusetts Institute of Technology. "But the concern here is that using a tactic like this, which may be more efficient than the pack and crack strategy, might further reduce minority representation."

The practice, ironically, took root 40 years ago, when then president Lyndon B. Johnson signed the Voting Rights Act. The landmark civil rights legislation was created to overcome a legacy of poll taxes, Whites-only primaries and literacy tests, especially in Southern states. But it wasn't long before its foes began designing ways around it.

Intended and Unintended Consequences

Lawmakers and scholars agree that politics has changed in two fundamental ways since the authorization of the Voting Rights Act: Blacks exercise their voting power and hold political office in great numbers, and Republicans, with almost no Black support, are the dominant party both nationally and in the South.

The two aren't unrelated. Republican gains came partly through redrawing political boundaries and packing as many African Americans into as few districts as possible in the early 1990s. The plan increased the number of Black representatives in Congress but bolstered GOP gains in the surrounding districts.

Democratic strategist Matt Angle credits the practice with nearly doubling the number of Black and Hispanic representatives elected to Congress in the past decade. But the boost has come at his party's peril. He calls it "the unholy alliance."

"Democrats are scared to death to deal honestly with issues in respect to race," says Angle, a former congressional aide and founder of the Lone Star Project, a political action committee that monitors Republican activities. "White and

Black Democrats couldn't figure out how to work together, and that allowed Republicans to come in and pack districts. They're still doing it, and that's going to kill us."

"When minority voters really start to be effective at the polls, Republicans change the rules and move the ball," Angle says. "It's a cynical view of the law to lessen the impact of minority voters. This isn't a matter of racism, it's about power. It's how power protects power."

Spencer A. Overton, a law professor at George Washington University who specializes in voting rights and who served on the Jimmy Carter-James Baker Commission on Federal Election Reform, says political elites from both parties are harming voters of all persuasions.

"Our voting rights are under attack by incumbent politicians of both parties who manipulate rules in order to win elections," says Overton. "These rules include redistricting, they also include English-only ballots, antiquated voting machines, photo identification and a whole host of other devices." Overton's recently released book, *Stealing Democracy: The New Politics of Voter Suppression*, examines modern methods of voter disenfranchisement.

This July [2006], the U.S. Congress renewed the Voting Rights Act for another 25 years, but the statute's survival is still in jeopardy. By federal law, Texas must get permission to change any of its election rules because of its history of minority voter disenfranchisement. But a small district in northwest Austin filed suit against the U.S. Department of Justice last month [September 2006], claiming that a key provision in the renewed act is unconstitutional.

U.S. Rep. Melvin L. Watt, D-N.C., one of the chief architects of the renewed legislation, says the Voting Rights Act has been legally challenged almost every year since its inception. This is no different, he says.

The revised law seeks to restore the Voting Rights Act to its original strength. Many supporters say it has been weakened over the years by U.S. Supreme Court decisions regarding redistricting. While some Republicans, primarily from Southern states, sought to "reform" the new bill, other Republicans joined forces with Black leaders to assure its passage.

As long as White citizens refuse to vote for candidates of other races and ethnicities, districts that ensure Blacks and Hispanics will elect candidates of their choice are needed, advocates say. That's why Black leaders are aligning themselves with Republicans, says Kimberly Perkins, an assistant general counsel for the NAACP [National Association for the Advancement of Colored People] who specializes in redistricting and voting rights.

"Republicans have been our friends in some respects by creating majority-minority districts," she says. "On the other hand, Democrats tend to bring more of our issues to the table. I don't know who's got it right, and I don't know that we've come up with the perfect plan. I do know that minority interests are being traded off. I'm just not sure how we stop it."

Crossing the Line

This fall's mid-term elections are important to watch in part because they will help set the stage for redistricting battles to come in 2011, says Dr. Michael P. McDonald, a visiting fellow at the Brookings Institution and an assistant professor of government and politics at George Mason University in Fairfax, Va.

"Whoever controls the state legislature or key positions in state government controls the political landscape for the entire decade," he says. "Partisan battles in the redistricting war start right now. Republicans get it. Democrats are just starting to get it."

In the past, legislators drew their maps using markers, paper maps and adding machines, but the process was time consuming and often inaccurate. Today, computer consultants hired by politicians know exactly where minority voters live, says Dr. Mark J. Salling, an expert in election demographics with the Center for Election Integrity at Cleveland State University. With the click of a mouse, politicians can move lines on computer screens and create the perfect proportion of Black, White or Hispanic voting blocs to achieve a predetermined outcome, he says.

During the late 1980s and 1990s, politicians and their consultants combined U.S. Census tracts to produce the racial makeup they wanted for a district, Salling says. "Now they can build districts household by household by clicking on neighborhood blocks and finding out how many registered voters live there, the race of the people inside each house and how each of them voted in the last three elections."

With that information in hand, legislators can now predict how each household is going to vote, Salling says, "and draw the line exactly the way the politician wants it."

Texas, where Davis lives, isn't the worst offender of manipulating boundary lines; it's just gotten the most attention lately. The efforts of Republicans to secure more seats in Congress by redrawing boundaries led protesting Democrats to flee to Oklahoma to avoid ratifying the new districts. U.S. Rep. Tom DeLay, one of the plan's chief architects, was forced to give up his position as Speaker of the House, and eventually his seat in Congress, after being indicted for allegedly violating campaign finance laws in a fund-raising scheme that was part of his redistricting plot.

Fighting Battles Nationwide

Political leaders in other states have fought similar battles. In California, for example, Democrats drew lines that protected their incumbents, much to the chagrin of activists who thought the surge in the Hispanic population presented a chance to draw new lines to boost Hispanic representation. Republicans challenged the new map, but the state Supreme

Minorities Gained from 1990s Redistricting

Race-conscious redistricting in the 1990s contributed to a marked increase in the number of blacks and Hispanics elected to the U.S. House of Representatives. But recent Supreme Court decisions now limit legislatures' discretion to create so-called "majority-minority" districts.

African-American and Hispanic Members of U.S. House of Representatives

Year	Blacks	Hispanics
1991	26	11
2001	37	19
2003	37	22

TAKEN FROM: CQ.com, *CQ Weekly, American Political Leaders: 1789–2000,* CQ Press.

Court decided it would stand. Ohio Republican strategist Jim Tilling recalls trying to draw fair boundary lines for his state, but GOP leaders—pressured by the state NAACP—forced him to pack Black voters into a district around Cleveland. Democrats sued, and the case went to the U.S. Supreme Court, which sided with the Republicans.

"It helped that I went before the Court with members of the NAACP standing next to me. That way, no one could say the map violated minority voting rights," Tilling says.

Creative line drawing in Franklin County, Ohio, is another example, Tilling says. Columbus, the county seat and the state capital, is led by a Black Democratic mayor. The area is also where Democratic presidential candidate John Kerry beat George W. Bush by almost 50,000 votes in the 2004 presidential election. But the districts for the congressional seats are drawn in such a way that Republicans hold all three of the county's seats in the U.S. House.

According to Friedman and Holden's study, the most gerrymandered maps in the country can be found in Florida,

Ohio and Pennsylvania. Last fall [2005], Ohio Democrats, with the exception of several African American leaders, fought to change the way political lines are drawn in their state. That effort was successfully beaten back by Republicans. But with abysmal GOP poll numbers suggesting that Democrats may sweep back into power, leaders from both parties are scrambling to change their respective tunes.

"When one political party is about to lose some power, fairness all of a sudden becomes a great value," says Dr. John C. Green, director of the University of Akron's Bliss Institute of Applied Politics. "If Republicans have suddenly realized the importance of fairness, Democrats have just as suddenly rediscovered the value of partisanship."

Davis hasn't felt that sense of fairness in her redrawn district in Texas. The political priorities in her Black, teetering middle-class neighborhood focus largely on crime, jobs and economic development. But her new Republican congressman, Michael C. Burgess, acknowledges that the mostly White and rural constituents that make up his base are more concerned about immigration and roads. He backs President [George W.] Bush's 2007 proposed budget, which cuts spending on higher education and Medicare—issues that have received strong support in the Black community. Before the redesign, Burgess's district was fairly compact. Now, it stretches 100 miles, from east Ft. Worth to the Oklahoma border. And as the district size has grown, the voting strength of Davis's neighborhood has dwindled.

"We don't have any interests in common," she says of Burgess. "He doesn't represent me. Rather than work to convert us, they just carved us out like we were nobodies."

Viewpoint

> *"It's hard to imagine the [Supreme Court] justices inventing a new right to more competitive districts, or where in the Constitution they could find it."*

The Supreme Court Appears Unlikely to Resolve Problems with Partisan Redistricting

Stuart Taylor

Although gerrymandering—changing electoral districts for political gain—has polarized politics, the U.S. Supreme Court is not likely to resolve the problem, argues Stuart Taylor in the following viewpoint. The Court has issued confusing and contradictory rulings on redistricting, he claims. While the Court has held that some gerrymanders might be unconstitutional, Taylor asserts, it has never struck one down nor set any standards for doing so. He maintains that dissenting justices have warned that an emphasis on one-person, one-vote policies and laws requiring "majority-minority" districts have had unintended consequences and may have encouraged gerrymandering. Taylor is a regular contributor to National Journal.

Stuart Taylor Jr., "The Trouble with Texas," *National Journal*, vol. 38, March 4, 2006, pp. 13–14.

As you read, consider the following questions:

1. In Stuart Taylor's view, why have moderates almost disappeared?
2. What famous Supreme Court justice does the author claim warned about court interference with redistricting and why?
3. According to the author, why are decisions striking down racial gerrymanders easily evaded by the Court?

A dispiriting reality sank in as the Supreme Court worked through two hours of arguments on March 1 [2006] about the egregious gerrymander that Tom DeLay helped ram through the Texas legislature in 2003: The Court has no intention of fixing—and no idea how to fix—the mess that it has made of our politics (with ample help from politicians) over more than four decades. And nobody else seems to have a good idea, either.

This mess is not just in Texas. Nor will it be ameliorated by whatever the Court does in the Texas case.[1] Not even in the highly unlikely event of a decision to strike down the congressional redistricting map that knocked off five Democratic incumbents in 2004, while delivering 21 of Texas's 32 House seats to Republicans, up from 15 in 2002.

The mess to which I refer is state legislatures' use of gerrymandering—manipulating election district lines to help or hurt a particular candidate or group—to make 80 to 90 percent of the nation's 435 House districts so lopsidedly Republican or Democratic that the out party has almost no chance of winning.

The paucity of competitive general elections for House seats, bad enough in itself, has also helped polarize our politics into the bitter liberal-conservative brawling that litters the

1. In June 2006, the Supreme Court upheld most of Texas's 2003 redistricting plan, giving a variety of reasons for rejecting the constitutional challenge.

landscape today. Primaries, dominated by the most fervently partisan voters, are the only real contests. So victory goes to the most liberal of Democrats and the most conservative of Republicans. Moderates, who used to grease the wheels of conciliation and compromise, have almost disappeared.

The polarization that has poisoned the House has also infected the Senate to a lesser extent. Senators run statewide. But many climbed the ladder by being liberal or conservative enough to win in gerrymandered House or state legislative districts.

There will never be a better opportunity than the Texas case for the Supreme Court to do something about this. This is not because of the much-publicized hijinks and other particulars of the DeLay-driven decision to draw new districts to defeat incumbent Democrats. It is because the case raises all of the big questions that bear on redistricting, and because it will be the first opportunity for Chief Justice John Roberts and Justice Samuel Alito to address them.

Are partisan gerrymanders ever unconstitutional? If so, how to decide how extreme is too extreme? How many black-controlled and Hispanic-controlled districts must the state create (or preserve) to satisfy the Voting Rights Act? Must states strive for proportional representation of racial groups? At what point do efforts to satisfy the Voting Rights Act collide with the Court's equal protection rules against drawing oddly shaped districts with race as a "predominant factor"?

The justices have made the law on all of these issues so confusing, so internally contradictory, and so mind-numbingly complex as to be almost incomprehensible. But neither Roberts nor Alito, nor any other justice, suggested any way for the Court to improve the situation much, probably because no way exists.

"Courts ought not to enter this political thicket," Justice Felix Frankfurter wrote 60 years ago. If he and the Warren Court's liberals are still in touch, Frankfurter must be saying,

"I told you so." The one-person, one-vote decisions of the early 1960s have had the unintended consequence of enabling politicians to choose their voters rather than the other way around.

Those decisions ended the gross malapportionment of congressional and legislative districts that had diluted the voting power of urban voters in much of the country. They also galvanized a national consensus that every vote should have equal weight. Indeed, when Alito was challenged during his confirmation hearing to explain a disapproving mention he made two decades ago of the reapportionment decisions, he had little choice but to endorse the one-person, one-vote principle as "a fundamental part of our constitutional law."

But Alito added a criticism of the Court for "taking it to extremes, requiring that districts be exactly equal in population, which did not seem to me to be a sensible idea." He was right.

So was Justice Lewis Powell, in a 1983 dissent warning that the Court's "uncompromising emphasis on numerical equality" would "encourage and legitimate even the most outrageously partisan gerrymandering." Requiring near-exact numerical equality made a hash of the traditional redistricting standards: city and county lines, compactness, contiguity, and the like. Those had been the only brakes on gerrymandering.

Later, the justices' unduly broad reading of the 1982 Voting Rights Act amendments as requiring safe seats for black and Latino politicians led to the drawing of oddly shaped "majority-minority" districts.

Politicians, under legal compulsion to draw oddly shaped districts, have pursued their own purposes while they were at it. Meanwhile, computer software has allowed the party in power to draw districts with exactly the desired numbers of Democrats and Republicans.

In California and other states, the two parties have collaborated to draw safe districts for as many incumbents as

Supreme Court Ruling May Pave the Way for Further Redistricting

The Supreme Court upheld most of Texas's Republican-drafted 2003 congressional redistricting plan [on June 28, 2006] in a ruling that could prompt majority parties in other states to redraw political maps to their advantage....

The seven justices [who formed the majority] gave widely varying reasons for rejecting the constitutional challenge [brought by opponents of the Texas plan], and the Court did not quite say that no such challenge could ever succeed.

But with six justices producing 123 pages of opinions, without any five of them able to agree on how to define an unconstitutional gerrymander, politicians of both parties said that the ruling leaves the door wide open to attempts to copy the [Republican U.S. representative Tom] DeLay strategy in other states.

Charles Lane and Dan Balz,
"Justices Affirm GOP Map for Texas,"
The Washington Post, *June 29, 2006.*

possible. This is bipartisan gerrymandering. In Texas and other states, the party in power has drawn maps designed to entrench its own incumbents while hurting those of the other party. That is partisan gerrymandering.

The Court has sought since 1993 to undo some of this damage by striking down a few especially bizarre-looking racial gerrymanders. But these decisions are easily evaded, both because they bump up against the Court's own Voting Rights Act rules and because the Court allows redistricters to pack mostly Democratic black voters into bizarrely shaped districts as long as the primary goal is to create safe Democratic districts.

Meanwhile, a bare majority of the Court has suggested that a sufficiently extreme partisan gerrymander might be unconstitutional, but the Court has never struck one down.

In 2003, in *Vieth v. Jubelirer*, the four more liberal justices wanted to strike down all or part of a 2002 gerrymander that had given Republicans 12 of the 19 House seats in Pennsylvania, which had more registered Democrats than Republicans. Four other justices said that the Court should never strike down a partisan gerrymander. Justice Anthony Kennedy, the deciding vote, said that no manageable definition of unfairness in redistricting had yet emerged, but he left the door open for future cases.

Which brings us to the 2003 Republican gerrymander in Texas. It is no more flagrant than the Pennsylvania gerrymander. Democrats, however, argue that it is uniquely outrageous because the legislature's only reason for drawing a new Texas map was partisan advantage.

The legislature did not need to redraw the map to comply with the one-person, one-vote rule, the Democrats stress, because a special three-judge federal district court had already done that in 2001. (The legislature had deadlocked in 2001 without adopting any map.) Ergo, say the Democrats, the newly Republican legislature's 2003 map was a purely partisan move to hurt Democratic incumbents and voters. Pretty persuasive, thinks I.

But wait: The state counters that it redrew the 2001 map to undo the lingering effects of a 1991 Democratic gerrymander. It enabled Democrats to win a 17–15 majority of the congressional delegation in 2002, even though Republicans had outpolled Democrats by 53 percent to 44 percent statewide. Even more persuasive, thinks I.

But wait again: The 2001 map had actually given Republicans an advantage in 20 of the 32 districts, say the Democrats. They held 17 seats in 2002 only because the advantage of incumbency had brought crossover votes from Republicans. That clinches it, I decided—until I was reminded that incumbents tend to keep running for life, so that the 2001 map might have perpetuated a Democratic majority in a 60 percent Republican state for the rest of the decade.

Perhaps you, dear reader, can clearly discern from all this what would be the fairest outcome. But I have given up. And most of the justices seemed content to leave bad enough alone. They also seemed likely to reject most or all of the Democrats' claims that this or that district had too few or too many voters of this or that race.

Whatever the outcome, it would be nice if the justices could tidy up a bit—bringing a dollop of clarity to their rules, loosening the one-person, one-vote straitjacket, reducing the pressure to draw minority-controlled districts even in places where minority candidates have a fair shot without such manipulations.

But it's hard to imagine the justices inventing a new right to more competitive districts, or where in the Constitution they could find it. Someone else will have to fix this mess. Otherwise, we will be stuck with it forever.

Periodical Bibliography

The following articles have been selected to supplement the diverse views presented in this chapter.

Aaron Brooks	"The Court's Missed Opportunity to Draw the Line on Partisan Gerrymandering: *Lulac v. Perry*," *Harvard Journal of Law & Public Policy*, Spring 2007.
John C. Courtney	"Electoral Districting in the U.S.: Can Canada Help?" *Issues in Governance Studies*, June 2008.
Marc Dunkelman	"Gerrymandering the Vote: How a 'Dirty Dozen' States Suppress as Many as 9 Million Voters," Democratic Leadership Council, June 2008.
Michael S. Kang	"Race and Democratic Contestation," *Yale Law Journal*, March 2008.
Charles Lane and Dan Balz	"Justices Affirm GOP Map for Texas: Other States May Follow Suit," *The Washington Post*, June 29, 2006.
Adam Mueller	"The Implications of Legislative Power: State Constitutions, State Legislatures, and Mid-Decade Redistricting," *Boston College Law Review*, 2007.
David G. Savage	"Supreme Court Skeptical About Preserving Voting Rights Act Provision," *Los Angeles Times*, April 29, 2009.
Mark Sherman	"Supreme Court Voting Rights Act Ruling: Court Refuses to Expand Minority Voting Rights," *The Huffington Post*, March 9, 2009.
The Washington Post	"Gridlock in the Forecast," August 18, 2008.
George Will	"Honor the Voting Rights Act by Retiring It," *Columbia Daily Tribune* [Missouri], January 19, 2009.

CHAPTER 4

What Recent Developments Have Most Influenced Political Campaigns?

Chapter Preface

Cyberpolitics, the use of the Internet to campaign for public office, came of age in the 2004 U.S. presidential election. Using the Internet as a campaign tool in early 2003 turned a relatively obscure presidential candidate, Howard Dean, into the Democratic-frontrunner. "The Internet was his rocket ship, and nobody can deny how far and how fast the rocket ship took him up," claims Phil Noble, publisher of *PoliticsOnline*. The 2004 campaign also saw the growth of the small campaign donor, which allowed Dean to compete with candidates who had greater access to wealthy donors. Although Dean's campaign stalled in January 2004, his Internet success led other political candidates and their supporters to take advantage of this new political campaign tool. While few dispute the significant role the Internet now plays in political campaigns, one of several controversies concerning the influence of recent developments in political campaigns is whether the Internet increases public access to the political process.

Some argue that the "digital divide," the gap between wealthy Americans who have Internet access and the poor and less educated who do not, prevents the Internet from truly leveling the political playing field. While the number of those with Internet access is increasing, they maintain, the divide itself has in fact grown. According to a 2007 Pew Center study, 56 percent of Latino adults and 60 percent of blacks access the Internet compared to 71 percent of whites. In response to claims that the price of Internet access is dropping, Pew researcher Amanda Lenhart laments, "IT's still significant for a household that is at or just above the poverty line." Relying on public access sites such as libraries is not the same as having home access, in her view. As more political campaigns move online, reasons Lenhart, "a subset of people are not participating in that dialogue." Larry Noble, of the Center for Responsive Politics, agrees. "When groups like ours look at using the Internet to reach people, we have to be aware there's still a whole segment of society that doesn't have daily access."

Other commentators claim that the digital divide does not prevent people from participating in the political process. Christine Iverson, former Republican National Committee press secretary, explains that the Internet is not the only form of political communication; thus the Internet does not remove low income or minority citizens from the political process. "There are so many other ways to reach out to voters—phone, mail, television—the Internet is just one component of an overall plan. If you don't reach a voter thorough one method, you'll do anything you can to reach the voter through another," she maintains. Veteran campaign manager Steve Murphy agrees. He argues that fears of the political impact of the digital divide are misplaced. Analysts once raised the same concerns with television. "I'm optimistic that computers will become a more integral part of everybody's life in the coming years," Murphy maintains.

Whether the Internet will increase public access and participation in the political process remains hotly contested. According to Wade Henderson, executive director of the Leadership Conference on Civil Rights, "In a perfect world, the notion that the Internet can democratize public information and one's ability to participate in the debate is very real. It is potentially the ultimate democratizing medium. But, in practice, not yet." The authors in the following chapter debate other controversies concerning the influence of political campaign developments.

Viewpoint 1

"The sophistication of the Internet is leading to a major transformation in political elections."

The Internet Has Revolutionized Political Campaigns

Janette Kenner Muir

The Internet has transformed political elections, asserts Janette Kenner Muir in the following viewpoint. Internet blogs and social networks have increased citizen engagement in the election process, she maintains. In fact, blogs add an additional level of transparency by increasing the dialogue among journalists, professors, and average citizens who check the veracity of political claims. Using e-mail and campaign Web sites, candidates can bypass traditional media and communicate directly with potential voters, creating armies of supporters, she claims. Muir is associate professor of interdisciplinary and integrative studies at George Mason University.

Janette Kenner Muir, "Closing the Gap: Media, Politics, and Citizen Participation," *Harvard International Review*, vol. 30, Spring 2008, pp. 54–57.

As you read, consider the following questions:

1. In Janette Kenner Muir's opinion, what impact does the growing voice of citizens on the Internet have on the media?
2. According to the author, what nation has the most vibrant blogging community in sub-Saharan Africa?
3. In the author's view, what does political literacy require?

It's primary election night in Manchester, New Hampshire. Bright lights of media tents beckon political thrill seekers, most of whom are trying to catch a glimpse of their favorite candidate or media celebrity. The lights cast an eerie glow on the dark night, as cameras, posed in various places, wait with anticipation. Important things are happening here in this snowy town, located in an ardently independent and politically active state. As election results are reported, political candidates begin to sort themselves out—the best rising to the top, the remainder wondering how much longer they can spend precious resources chasing a dream that only a few will ever achieve.

New Hampshire managed to retain its "First in the Nation" primary status in 2008, amidst attempts by other states to close in on this treasured position. Despite protestations from across the country, there is good reason for starting here. From the interplay of candidates and the press to the frenetic energy of campaign volunteers, no other state provides as many opportunities to see politics in action. As the political campaign process unfolds, there are numerous ways to directly connect with candidates, which is something that becomes increasingly difficult as the primary season progresses and the front-runners are anointed. This primary also provides an early view of the political energy associated with this campaign year, making it feel different from previous elections. One only needs to look around to see the myriad of political signs dotting the highway, dozens of people standing on street corners cheering for their favorite candidate, and the campaign buses and press trucks creating traffic jams to know that something profound is happening here. There seems to be a movement afoot, a passionate desire for change, and a hope for a new perspective. For some it is the search for a new conservative heart. For others it is the promise of a completely new direction for the country.

The Link Between Politics and the Media

In January [2008] I had the privilege of traveling to New Hampshire with 18 others for a course called, "On the Campaign Trail." Our goal was to see and learn about as many political candidates as possible and observe their relationships with media and potential voters. Spending a week trudging through snow, attending candidate events, and talking with the press and citizens alike, one cannot help but take away from that experience the firm realization that politics and media are inextricably linked. As with previous elections, the political reality that candidates attempt to create is directly wedded to the way that reality is mediated by journalists.

Politics and media are clearly intertwined in shaping the national political agenda. Adding to this complexity, however, is a greater public voice utilizing various means to engage citizen participants in the unfolding story. This year, citizen engagement is another strong source of influence, manifested through Internet social networks and blogging sites. As this voice grows, it becomes more challenging for media outlets to garner the kind of influence they held in past presidential campaign seasons. These challenges have significant implications for elections throughout the world.

Every campaign season generates discussion about the ways that media influence the political process and shape public debate. From the earliest US broadsides and editorial cartoons, media have played important roles in framing campaign issues and personalities. In US politics specifically, the press has gone through various stages of influence and now it faces perhaps it greatest identity crisis as it redefines its role in media-saturated society. . . .

Technological Development

The sophistication of the Internet is leading to a major transformation in political elections, particularly in the availability of information and the potential for active engagement in the process. Interactive technology is ushering in a whole new way of thinking about civic engagement in politics. One area of significant relevance is blogging. Often called "the Sixth Estate," bloggers—who can provide an added level of transparency to the process of reporting—are transforming how we access and absorb political news. Through careful fact checking, scathing critiques, and dialogue, these Web journals written by journalists, professors, and average citizens provide another layer of influence as they attempt to ensure that political claims are substantiated and well-developed.

Another technological development transforming the election process is the personalization of electronic messages between the candidate and potential voters. Through e-mail and Web sites, candidates can often bypass traditional media and directly interact with the public in an electronic form of direct mail that is relatively inexpensive and far more expedient. Candidates and their surrogates send daily e-mail messages to supporters and potential voters, keeping them apprised of critical moments, popularity surges, and the need to send more money to maintain momentum. Web sites such as Facebook and MySpace generate armies of political supporters willing to give money and work locally for their candidates. Electronic bulletin boards keep voters informed about candidate sightings and other political events. Given these technological developments and the ability of some political candidates to embrace these new technologies, it is easy to understand the growing interest among young people in this year's US presidential election and the increasing use of the Internet for gathering political information.

A Global Transformation

Evidence for shifting influences in media and increased citizen involvement can be found in the international arena as well. Throughout the world, political candidates are learning ways to stage political events for the largest possible influence, as gauged through media coverage and public attention. Looking at the elections in Russia, Pakistan, and Kenya further highlights this phenomenon.

Consider the visual snapshots of Vladimir Putin and his successor, Dmitry Medvedev, standing together for a mediated moment following the Russian presidential election [in March 2008]. The victory pose of these two leaders, aired throughout Russia and around the globe, illustrates the role visual power has in establishing authority and credibility for the incoming president. The message this image projects contrasts greatly with Russian bloggers' interpretations of this election and the subsequent government that will result. The uncritical media coverage of Putin's anointed predecessor angered many bloggers as they attempted to identify the characteristics of the first deputy prime minister and his relationship with Putin, while also pointing out the merits of other political candidates. Greater government control of the Russian news media through state-owned corporations and wealthy loyal investors has greatly influenced what ends up on Russian television. On the other hand, bloggers are significantly contributing to reporting the reality of the situation, often through the use of sarcasm and unfiltered remarks. Though Medvedev has won the election, there is evidence to suggest that the Kremlin may be concerned about the uncontrolled nature of the Internet and is considering legislation to regulate this kind of "extremist material."

The Voice of the People

Bloggers also responded to the [2008] election in Pakistan. Many Web sites captured the anger citizens felt toward US involvement in the election process, responding to editorials in Pakistani newspapers that accused the United States of meddling in the country's affairs. Web sites such as Voice of America News and Human Rights Watch provided stories underscoring the role of the people in changing the course of Pakistan's election. Though the election was a highly contentious one, the outcome represented a transformation in Pakistani politics that points to a more engaged citizenry.

Similarly, Kenya's blogging community has been praised as one of the most vibrant in sub-Saharan Africa. Over 60 blog sites devoted specifically to the Kenyan election process discuss the violence and unrest that have resulted from perceived fraudulent activities, involving vote tabulations that put incumbent president Mwai Kibaki back in power [in 2008]. When the government instituted a media blackout, blogs were critical in spreading the latest news. Even after the blackout was lifted, bloggers were faster and more detailed in their reporting about the latest clashes than were other news sources. Blogs, along with mobile phones, are attempting to tell the story in ways that reflect the pain and struggle of the Kenyan people.

While critics will argue that access to the Internet is still minimal in many countries—with limited numbers of personal computers, slow connections, and a complete lack of access in poorer areas—the Internet's influence and potential to reach people has only just begun to be explored in many societies. The amazing growth of public voices telling the stories that most of the world does not get to see speaks to the tremendous potential the Internet has in shaping future campaigns and elections. One can only imagine the possibilities for future elections as more and more people acquire better access to technology. As this access grows, so does the poten-

tial for elections to run in a more fair and open manner. Information is ubiquitous and expansive. While various countries may struggle with reaching the electorate, there are many media outlets, converging on the Internet, that play important roles in disseminating news about the political process.

What of the Future?

As influence continues to shift, politics and media converge on new technologies. Given these realities, campaigns must continue to seek out the simplest and most effective ways to transmit and receive messages. In turn, media outlets must consider multiple ways to feed consumers and new ways to maintain viability. In 2008, candidates have found growing support in online social networks such as Facebook and MySpace. There are even Facebook groups formed to support Kenyan peace efforts and efforts to create a Russian version of Facebook. The Pakistani Facebook claims over 145,000 friends in its network [and] includes all sorts of commentary and YouTube videos. These networks are bound to continue their growth and influence in future elections.

Increasing Political Literacy and Civil Discourse

As consumers of politics, we can increase our political literacy by becoming more aware of these integrated systems. We can learn how to analyze the ways candidates shape messages to acquire media attention and how media outlets support much of this shaping. Political literacy requires that we understand the economics of the process as well as the ways persuasive messages are created and sustained. It also means that we need to dig deeper to address the short attention spans of the public and encourage people to grapple with the actual ideas of the candidate.

A positive feature that results this year from observing US politics and the rise of public voices in presidential campaigns is the creation of a more civil discourse that attempts to bypass more mediated environments to directly respond to individual concerns. As the pool of presidential candidates evolves, it will become increasingly necessary to determine the best ways to address race, gender, class, and religious differences in a manner that advances constructive political dialogue. The transparency of blogging may help to keep discourse on a civil level—or at the very least, bloggers will challenge unfair claims on all sides of the political spectrum and tell the stories that need to be heard. There is hope that with the right access, political transparency will continue to spread worldwide.

Does the art of political persuasion still exist? One need only look to the sweeping oratory of Barack Obama, the careful event staging of John McCain, or the one-on-one interpersonal style of Hillary Clinton to know that there is clearly an art to doing it right. The rhetoric may not always be aesthetically pleasing, but it is intentional, creative, and passionate. Journalistic reports of politics must take into account these same needs to persuade and inspire, and the Internet is becoming the place where citizens can lend their voice to the public debate. Democracy is not a perfect system; it can be a messy construct. But politics and media are permanent businesses in American society that will continue to evolve with time, technological advances, and true believers.

VIEWPOINT 2

> *"It's only a matter of time before voter suppression tactics make the leap to the Internet."*

The Internet Makes It Easier to Spread Campaign Misinformation

Julian Sanchez

While political misinformation and voter suppression campaigns might look a little different in an online context, the tactics will be basically the same as they have been in the past, claims Julian Sanchez in the following viewpoint. Young people, the largest population to seek political information online, will likely be the primary targets of such campaigns, he asserts. Internet campaign and election scammers will likely use tools such as hijacking or spoofing official campaign or local election board sites, Sanchez maintains. The greatest threat is that Internet scams can be disseminated close to Election Day, making it difficult for candidates to correct false information. Sanchez writes for the technology news site Ars Technica *and* Reason *magazine.*

As you read, consider the following questions:

1. What does Julian Sanchez claim are some of the voter suppression techniques that crop up like clockwork during election season?
2. What does the author assert are the best lies?
3. What legislation would criminalize the intentional spread of false election information for the purpose of vote suppression, according to the author?

Make sure your driving record is clear, citizen. See that you've paid off your parking tickets and paid up your child support, and remembered to bring two forms of ID before showing up to the polls on Thursday. That's the preposterous, predictable refrain of the voter "information" flyers and robocalls that crop up like clockwork—usually in minority neighborhoods—during election season, touting ersatz endorsements, fictitious voting requirements, and precisely wrong times, dates, and places at which to make your voice heard in the democratic process. With old-fashioned smear campaigns already proving disturbingly effective in digital form, civil rights activists worry that it's only a matter of time before voter suppression tactics make the leap to the Internet. Earlier this week [May 2008], at the annual Computers, Freedom and Privacy conference, they braced for the inevitable.

As NAACP [National Association for the Advancement of Colored People] attorney Jenigh Garrett explained, traditional vote suppression campaigns often targeted African American communities. African American voters have for decades supported Democrats by huge margins, making race a reasonable proxy for partisanship, while geographic clustering makes it possible to contain the misinformation. The best lies often contain some small kernel of truth, making them seem more plausible to their intended audience. So often, Garrett noted, voter suppression fliers capitalize on the combination of aggressive policing practices and high incarceration rates in urban black neighborhoods, as well as the fact that many states do disenfranchise felons, to attempt to persuade potential voters that *any* interaction with the law renders them ineligible.

Online misinformation campaigns, panelists suggested, would necessarily look different in some respects, but are likely to operate on many of the same fundamental principles as their real-space precursors. Tech strategist Jon Pincus, campaign software entrepreneur John Aristotle Phillips, and Lillie Coney of the Electronic Privacy Information Center [EPIC] discussed a variety of tactics we're likely to see deployed—perhaps as early as November. Young people—who have been turning out in large numbers for Barack Obama, and who disproportionately seek their information online—would be likely targets, most believed, though online affinity groups and social networks would also permit targeted messaging.

Taking a cue from phishing con artists, political scammers might seek to hijack or spoof the official sites of campaigns or local election boards, giving their misinformation an added veneer of credibility. Similarly, spoofed e-mails could be employed to persuade recipients that information is coming from a trusted source. In addition to conventional denial of service attacks, the Internet might also be used to facilitate distributed phone-jamming, of the sort often used to disrupt get-out-the-vote efforts.

The Internet offers some distinct advantages for both voter suppression campaigns and their opponents. The timing of misinformation efforts is vital: The bad information needs to be disseminated relatively close to Election Day, with enough lead time to be spread to voters, but not enough for opponents to employ countermeasures. The speed of online communications allows scammers far greater precision on this front, but also allows for the rapid collation and correction of false information. Campaigns targeted by deceptive flyers often aren't even aware of their existence until it's too late. Simi-

Where the Public Learns About the Presidential Campaign

	Campaign Year		
Regularly learn something from...	**2000** %	**2004** %	**2008** %
Local TV news	48	42	40
Cable news networks	34	38	38
Nightly network news	45	35	32
Daily newspaper	40	31	31
Internet	**9**	**13**	**24**
TV news magazines	29	25	22
Morning TV shows	18	20	22
National Public Radio	12	14	18
Talk radio	15	17	16
Cable political talk	14	14	15
Sunday political TV	15	13	14
Public TV shows	12	11	12
News magazines	15	10	11
Late-night talk shows	9	9	9
Religious radio	7	5	9
C-SPAN	9	8	8
Comedy TV shows	6	8	8
Lou Dobbs Tonight	—	—	7

TAKEN FROM: Pew Research Center, October 31, 2008.

larly, the social networks that are apt to make such attractive targets for deceptive tactics also create fora for the exposure of these tactics. And while well-planned campaigns should be effectively untraceable, less competent scammers may leave electronic trails that can be traced.

Also on hand at the panel was Rachana Bhowmik, legislative counsel for Barack Obama, who touted the senator's Deceptive Practices and Voter Intimidation Prevention Act, which has passed the House of Representatives but stalled in the Senate. The bill would criminalize the knowing dissemination of false election information for the purpose of vote suppression, though in order to avoid encroaching on protected political speech (parody, for example), certain forms of misinformation, such as bogus endorsements, are not covered. While the law would not necessarily deter deceptive tactics, Bhowmik hopes it would at least convince journalists that such misinformation campaigns were newsworthy.

Until then, be sure to check Snopes [a Web site resource for validating and debunking urban legends, Internet rumors, and e-mail scams] before you head to the polls. You can take care of the parking tickets later.

VIEWPOINT 3

> *"The recent flood of Internet donations . . . is accomplishing what Watergate-era campaign-finance regulations set out to do: dilute the influence of special interests and wealthy donors."*

Small Internet Donors Can Make a Big Impact on Elections

Mary Jacoby

Internet donors have done what decades of campaign financing laws failed to do, claims The Wall Street Journal *staff writer Mary Jacoby in the following viewpoint. Small Internet donors have diluted the influence of large, special interest donors, she asserts. Public financing, designed to reduce the influence of large donors, imposes strict spending limits that are inadequate today, Jacoby maintains. The explosion of small donors, however, may make even public financing obsolete. Democratic candidates have best exploited the Internet donor boom, but Republican analysts hope to develop the small donor–Internet connection, Jacoby explains.*

As you read, consider the following questions:

1. What do Hillary Clinton's donation statistics show about running a major campaign, in Mary Jacoby's opinion?
2. According to political strategist David All, what is Obama creating with his campaign Web site and small donor videos?
3. In support of what types of campaigns is Internet giving growing, in the author's view?

The recent flood of Internet donations that has helped pump 2008 presidential campaign coffers to highs also is accomplishing what Watergate-era campaign-finance regulations set out to do: dilute the influence of special interests and wealthy donors.

The Small Donor Boom

The main beneficiaries of the boom in small donors are Democratic contenders Sens. Barack Obama and Hillary Clinton. Both were expected to file reports with the Federal Election Commission [FEC] Thursday night, detailing their February fund-raising. The Obama campaign has released numbers indicating the Illinois senator would report raising about $55 million in February, a one-month record for a primary candidate. About 90% of the total came from donors who gave increments of $100 or less.

New York Sen. Clinton also has seen a jump in small donations: For the $35 million she received in February, the average donation was about $100, and about 80% came over the Internet, campaign officials said. In January, 35% of her money came from donors giving $200 or less, compared with 16% from such donors in the last three months of 2007, according to the nonpartisan Campaign Finance Institute in Washington. "I think what it shows is you can run major campaigns on small donations. The Internet makes it more possible," said Brad Smith, a former Republican chairman of the FEC, and now chairman of the Center for Competitive Politics, a conservative legal organization in Alexandria, Va.

Wealthy donors who bundle contributions to candidates from friends and employees remain important. They provided the bulk of the early money for the Obama and Clinton campaigns. Beyond the Clinton-Obama battle, the technology that lets candidates reap millions from small donors hasn't caught fire. Sen. John McCain, the presumptive Republican nominee, hasn't seen such a jump in small donors. Nor have many congressional candidates. The Internet "has the potential over time to revolutionize the way campaigns are financed. But we're not there by any means," said Fred Wertheimer, an advocate of laws that restrict the amount of money federal candidates can raise and spend in an election.

The surge in small Web donations comes as the three-decade-old rules for public financing of presidential campaigns are fraying. The system, designed to ensure that candidates have enough resources to make their case to voters and to encourage them to seek small donations, uses taxpayer money to match the first $250 a campaign raises from each donor. But for candidates in the primaries, it imposes strict spending limits that Congress never indexed to inflation, leading some candidates to shun public funding as inadequate.

Creating a Community

For general elections, the government makes a lump-sum grant to the two major party candidates—this year, $85 million. No nominee has ever opted out of the general-election public system, but Sen. Obama is considering it. "We have built the kind of organization that is funded by the American people. That is exactly the goal and the aim of everybody who's interested in good government and politics," Sen. Obama said in a Feb. 26 debate.[1]

1. Barack Obama opted out of the public financing system for the 2008 general presidential election.

Political strategists are trying to replicate the Obama model. David All, a Republican political consultant, admired how the campaign last year chose five small donors to have dinner with Sen. Obama, and then made a video about each one and posted them to the Obama campaign Web site. "It told their story, and Barack Obama was merely the thread that connected them all," Mr. All said. "What he's doing is creating a community, and this community is spreading his message virally" by word of mouth and e-mails to friends, he said.

When Sen. Clinton launched her campaign just over a year ago, she focused much more on traditional fund-raisers and big givers who can donate the $2,300 maximum. That sent an early message that "you can do it all on the basis of $2,300 contributions raised by people who enlist only friends who can also give $2,300," said Michael Malbin of the Campaign Finance Institute, which is affiliated with George Washington University. "But then you're sending the strong message that a $50 contribution doesn't matter," he said.

Small Donor Campaign Dynamics

In the first nine months of 2007, 28% of donations to the Obama war chest came from people who gave $200 or less, compared with 13% for the Clinton campaign. By the last three months of 2007, the Obama number jumped to 47%, compared with 16% for the Clinton campaign. But the dynamics of the race changed early this year; Sen. Clinton came in third in the Iowa caucuses and spent heavily to win the New Hampshire primary in January and several important states Feb. 5. Her donors had mostly given $2,300, and Sen. Clinton announced she had lent her cash-strapped campaign $5 million.

The Clinton campaign put up an appeal on its Web site for $3 million. "We knew something was happening when we quickly exceeded that goal," said Peter Daou, Internet director for the Clinton campaign. In February, more than 200,000 do-

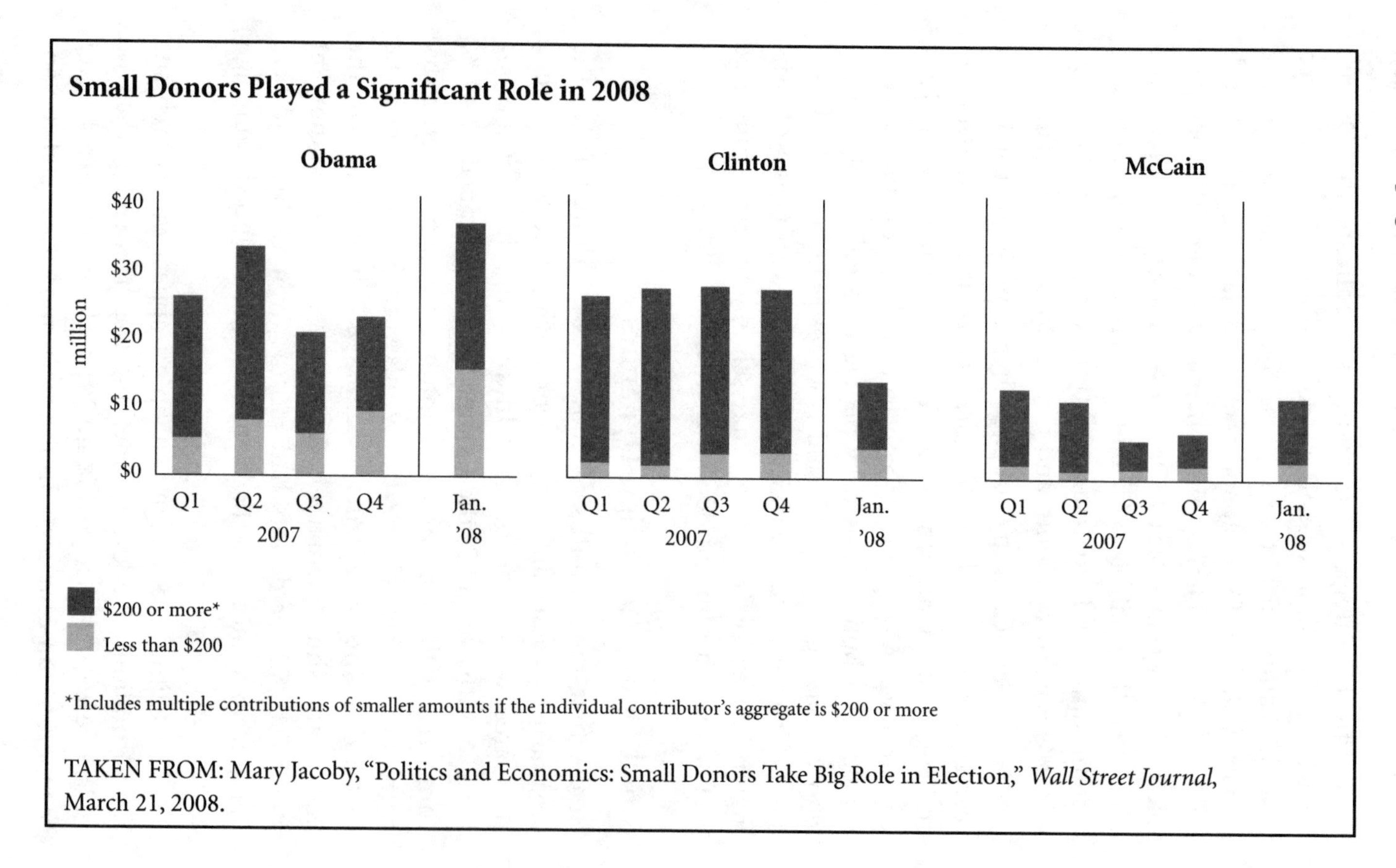

Small Donors Played a Significant Role in 2008

*Includes multiple contributions of smaller amounts if the individual contributor's aggregate is $200 or more

TAKEN FROM: Mary Jacoby, "Politics and Economics: Small Donors Take Big Role in Election," *Wall Street Journal*, March 21, 2008.

nors gave to Sen. Clinton for the first time, using credit and debit cards over the Internet. Her total take: $35 million in February.

First-time donor Sarah Reagosa, a college student in New Jersey, gave $10 through her debit card in February and then gave another $15. "Her being a woman makes me realize I can go out and overcome all the obstacles, just like she did," said Ms. Reagosa.

Internet giving at the congressional level also is spreading, albeit more slowly. Web sites such as ActBlue, a political action committee that supports Democrats, let donors contribute to individual candidates. ActBlue has directed more than $14 million to federal Democratic candidates this election cycle, compared with $16 million for the 2006 congressional elections.

Mr. All, the Republican consultant, started a rival site last October [2007] called Slatecard.com. It has raised just $300,000. "What I'm finding is a lot of Republican campaigns are just hiring college kids or using their son who has a Facebook account," said the 28-year-old Mr. All. "They don't understand what this is all about."

VIEWPOINT 4

"[Barack Obama's private fund-raising is] a model for the future—a future of ever-larger campaign war chests, but built from a far greater number of small, individual contributors."

Small Donor Fund-Raising Is Reshaping Campaign Finance

Kevin Diaz

The success of Barack Obama's small donor fund-raising and his decision to opt out of public financing may change the way presidential candidates pay for their campaigns, maintains Minneapolis Star Tribune *staff writer Kevin Diaz in the following viewpoint. Obama was the first major candidate to opt out of public financing since the program began, Diaz explains. Because of Obama's success, reform advocates are looking to create a new system that will focus on small donors, Diaz claims. Reform opponents, however, claim that the small donor revolution makes finance reform unnecessary, putting to rest concerns about corruption.*

Kevin Diaz, "Campaign Rewrites Fundraising Playbook," *Star Tribune* (Minneapolis, MN), November 3, 2008. Reproduced with permission of Star Tribune, Minneapolis-St. Paul.

As you read, consider the following questions:

1. According to Kevin Diaz, how did John McCain manage to stay close to Barack Obama in overall financial backing?
2. How do reform advocates plan to make small donors part of the campaign finance system, in the author's view?
3. Who do reform advocates blame for the failed public financing system, according to the author?

Barack Obama's staggering success raising money on the Internet, combined with the Democrat's decision to forgo public financing, has forced campaign analysts of all stripes to reexamine how to pay for future presidential campaigns.

Reexamining Campaign Finance

Not least among them is [2008] Republican hopeful John McCain, who was being outspent 3 to 2 in the final weeks of the campaign. He lamented Wednesday [October 29, 2008] on CNN: "You tell me the next time . . . a presidential candidate will take public financing when Senator Obama has shown you can raise millions of dollars."

Obama, the first major candidate since 1972 to use only private money in the general election, termed his decision "difficult" and blamed it on a public financing system that he says is "broken."

Critics say his record $639 million fund-raising total so far—compared with McCain's $360 million—could very well be the end of a public financing system that has prevailed for the past 34 years.

"It's a mess," said John Samples, a campaign finance scholar for the Cato Institute, a libertarian think tank in Washington, D.C., speaking of the public financing system. "It's certainly not serving any of the purposes it was supposedly set up to do."

Minnesotans, who rank 24th in donating to presidential candidates, have contributed a total of $10.5 million to all candidates throughout the primaries and the general election, according to the Center for Responsive Politics. Of that, more than $5.4 million has gone to Obama, compared with $2.3 million to McCain.

McCain, who has been limited to an $84.1 million public financing grant in the general election since the Republican National Convention, has managed to stay close to Obama in overall financial backing. That's been largely because of a number of legal loopholes on joint committees and the fund-raising success of the Republican National Committee, which, like its Democratic counterpart, can raise and spend money for ads geared to the presidential race.

A New Public System?

But if some see Obama's private fund-raising advantage as the death of public financing, others see it as a model for the future—a future of ever-larger campaign war chests, but built from a far greater number of small, individual contributors.

"Sen. Obama's campaign made an extraordinary breakthrough in small donor fund-raising on the Internet," said Fred Wertheimer, president and CEO of Democracy 21, which has been involved in drafting campaign finance reform legislation with Obama's backing. "That is the pathway to the future."

As Republicans have accused Obama of breaking a pledge to abide by public financing limits, he has talked of creating a "parallel public financing system" of turbocharged Internet contributions.

The Illinois senator has raised nearly $300 million from a list of more than 3 million ordinary donors giving less than $200 each, much of it over the Internet. While that sounds like "small-d" democracy, it represents less than half of his total haul. He's also raised about $200 million in contributions

A Backward Step or Leveling the Field?

Is something rotten in the state of public financing for presidential campaigns?. . .

Critics argue that the fact that Obama raised a record-smashing $153 million in September [2008] and has drawn in more money than any candidate in history is a backward step in campaign finance reform. . . .

But others see Obama's success as an attempt to level the campaign-funding playing field.

Millions of donors giving relatively small amounts—as opposed to large interest groups giving unlimited amounts—is, arguably, further democratization of the process. The Obama campaign reports it had 632,000 new donors in September, and the average gift was less than $100.

Linton Weeks,
"Did Obama Kill Public Campaign Finance?"
NPR, October 22, 2008.

of $1,000 or more, the type that are often associated with influential bundlers, expensive fund-raisers, and special access to the candidate.

Reform advocates see the potential for a system that would emphasize donations of less than $200 by matching them with public dollars at a ratio of 4 to 1 or more. Combined with spending limits for opting into public financing, that could produce large numbers of small contributions on the Internet that would quickly crowd out bigger donations from the rich.

"If the incentives are strong enough, the system will focus on the small donor and move away from the bundlers," said Wertheimer, who is working on a bill with Sen. Russ Feingold, the Wisconsin Democrat who teamed up with McCain after the 2000 elections to pass a ban on unlimited campaign contributions by corporations, unions and rich donors to political parties.

While Obama has signed on as a co-sponsor of Feingold's new public financing bill, McCain has not. And it remains to be seen what kind of support it would garner in the next Congress.

Feingold, in a statement Thursday to the *Star Tribune*, said he expects bipartisan support for his bill, adding that the public financing system "clearly needs to be updated if it is to remain viable".

An Unusual Candidate

Opponents of campaign finance reform point to Obama's fund-raising success as evidence that the whole idea of limiting campaign cash has become obsolete.

Bradley Smith, a former Federal Election Commission chairman, wrote in *The Washington Post* last week that Obama's effort should "put to rest all the shibboleths about campaign finance reform—that it's needed to prevent corruption, that it equalizes the playing field, or that tax subsidies are needed."

Some of Minnesota's biggest political contributors fall on opposite sides of the debate. Former U.S. Sen. Mark Dayton, an heir of the department store-owning family, said in a recent interview that the influence of big money "warps the decision-making process in Washington on behalf of the moneyed and special interests."

But Twin Cities [Minneapolis - St. Paul] businessman and Democratic political strategist Vance Opperman believes that campaign giving, as long as it's transparent, should be unlimited. Funding restrictions, he said, "signal to people that there's something awful and dirty and terrible about giving to political campaigns and parties. The reverse ought to be true."

Between January 2007 and Election Day [November 4, 2008], more than $2.4 billion will have been spent by all the presidential campaigns in this race, according to the Center for Responsive Politics. Not everyone agrees that's too much money.

But if Obama maintains his current lead in the polls and wins the election, some critics say, his private fund-raising advantage over the publicly financed McCain could become a prelude to the future.

"In the next couple of election cycles, [accepting public financing] could just be a signal that your campaign is dead, and the media will report it that way," Samples said.

Reformers say that could be fixed by raising the spending limits for candidates who accept public financing, something they blame Congress for not doing in recent years.

But even advocates of a system that encourages small donations say it remains to be seen if Obama's success on the Internet is an aberration or a harbinger of elections to come.

"Obama is an unusual candidate," said Steve Weissman, a researcher with the Campaign Finance Institute, a Washington-based watchdog group. "Others equally worthy may not have the charisma to generate the enthusiasm he's developed."

For Samples, the worst-case scenario is that the system is neither changed nor abolished: "The great danger is that it becomes a typical government program, in which it doesn't function, but it also doesn't go out of existence. It just sort of stays there."

Viewpoint 5

> "The idea that small donors will somehow reinvigorate electoral democracy . . . is attractive but not yet reality."

Small Donor Fund-Raising Will Not Change Campaign Finance

Jay Mandle

Despite claims of a small donor revolution, Jay Mandle argues in the following viewpoint that large donors still play a significant role in presidential campaigns. A closer look at Barack Obama's campaign reveals that in addition to seeking smaller donations, he also courted wealthy contributors. Mandle maintains that even Obama's small donors have more money than the average American. Small donors will not make elections fair and candidates accountable without major campaign finance reforms, he concludes. Mandle, an economics professor at Colgate University, is author of Democracy, America, and the Age of Globalization.

As you read, consider the following questions:

1. According to Jay Mandle, why can't we rely on the candidates' rhetoric to match the facts when it comes to small donors?

Jay Mandle, "The Small-Donor Fallacy," *The Washington Post*, June 20, 2008, p. A19. Reproduced by permission of the author.

2. Who does the author claim was one of Barack Obama's big donors?
3. Why did Obama reject public financing, in the author's view?

Not long ago, Sen. Barack Obama criticized special-interest lobbies that "use their money and influence to stop us from reforming health care or investing in renewable energy for yet another four years." He has said that his army of small donors constitutes "a parallel public financing system," one in which ordinary voters "will have as much access and influence over the course of our campaign" as that "traditionally reserved for the wealthy and the powerful."

Obama has raised record-breaking sums from small donors, so his announcement yesterday [June 19, 2008] that he would opt out of the public financing system for the general election did not surprise many. And the idea that the Internet and grassroots donations will somehow reinvigorate our democracy is appealing. But this notion is not borne out by the evidence.

The Importance of Big Donors

As of April 30 [2008], the Obama campaign had collected more than $120 million in contributions of $200 or less. In April alone, the latest month for which data are available, Obama raised more than $31 million, about 65 percent of which came from contributions of $200 or less. This seems good for democracy—but it may not be as good as we think.

Despite the importance of small donors, both Obama and Republican Sen. John McCain are still taking lots of big donations from wealthy special interests. In fact, when the nominating system as a whole is studied over time, the evidence suggests that the role of big donors will turn out to be growing, not shrinking.

Political Giving at a Glance

- *Individuals* are by far the largest source of federal funds for party committees. Republican committees reported receiving $246.3 million from individuals (86% of their receipts), while Democrats received $210.5 million (77% of their total).

- *The Bipartisan Campaign Reform Act (BCRA)* increased the contribution limit for individuals giving to national parties to $25,000, adjusted for inflation. The inflation-adjusted limit for the 2007–2008 election cycle is $28,500. All national committees, except the Democratic Senatorial Campaign Committee [DSCC], receive more dollars from donations in amounts less than $200 than from contributions in any other category.

- *Political Action Committees (PACs)* and other committees contributed $30.2 million to Republican Party committees and $49.4 million to Democratic Party committees in 2007–2008. Much of this total comes from House Democrats who contributed $22.5 million from their campaign accounts to the Democratic Congressional Campaign Committee [DCCC]. House Republicans contributed $11.6 million to the National Republican Congressional Committee [NRCC].

Thomas J. Billitteri,
"Campaign Finance Reform,"
CQ Researcher, *vols. 18–22, June 13, 2008.*

Through March [2008], small donations amounted to 39 percent of the combined fund-raising of Obama and Sen. Hillary Clinton. But over a comparable period four years ago, such contributions made up an even greater share (42 percent) of the fund-raising of the two leading Democratic contenders, Sen. John Kerry and former Vermont governor Howard Dean. On the GOP side, small donors were much more important for McCain in 2007 than they were for George W. Bush in 2003. But for most of last year McCain was not the front-runner, and his campaign was famously broke. Now that he is the presumptive nominee, big donors are his bread and butter.

Contributions of less than $200 do not have to be itemized in reports to the Federal Election Commission, so we have no idea how many are made. We also cannot rely on the candidates' rhetoric to match the facts. During a Feb. 26 [2008] debate in Cleveland, for example, Obama said that "we have now raised 90 percent of our donations from small donors, $25, $50." His campaign's own data from January 2007 through January 2008 show that 36 percent of donated funds were from small donors. Obama probably meant that 90 percent of the individuals who contributed were small donors, but the number of donors has not been verified.

Small-dollar donations to Obama have surged this year [2008], and those donors became crucial in the spring as the battle to secure the Democratic nomination intensified. But for most of his campaign, big donors have been Obama's mainstay. Employees of investment bank Goldman Sachs, for example, have contributed more than $570,000 to his campaign.

Campaign Finance Reform Is Still Necessary

Another problem with asserting that small donors are an antidote to undue influence by wealthy contributors is that even small donors are almost certainly much richer than the average American.

In a study of $100 contributions to state campaigns in six states during 2005, the Campaign Finance Institute found that more than half of donors earned between $75,000 and $250,000 a year. The median U.S. income that year was $46,000. While it's tricky to extrapolate to the presidential race, it is unlikely that campaign giving has suddenly become a common pursuit of working-class families.

Meanwhile, big-ticket fund-raising among the very wealthiest is surging into record territory. Even as he touts his base of small donors, Obama has continued to woo large contributors at events costing thousands of dollars per plate, as has McCain. This suggests that, by themselves, small donations do not offer a real corrective to the pay-to-play system.

Neither does the public financing available to the candidates. This funding is frozen at 1976 levels, which is why Obama has rejected it—he can raise from private sources more than the amount of the government grant. McCain no doubt would have taken the same path if his fund-raising had taken off.

The idea that small donors will somehow reinvigorate electoral democracy, without the trouble of fundamentally reforming our campaign finance laws, is attractive but not yet reality. For candidates to be equally responsive to all their constituents and to open to ordinary voters the same kind of influence and access now afforded a wealthy minority, the only realistic option is to increase the amount of money we allocate to the public campaign finance system. In fact, the small-donor illusion may even be functioning as a fig leaf, averting our gaze from the continued and intensifying stranglehold that big donors have on our democracy.

> *"Will the legions of small donors . . . be summoned to send e-mails to Congress and the media on behalf of the election mandate?"*

Small Donors May Influence Campaigns Beyond Financing

Michael Cornfield

Barack Obama's small donor revolution may signal more than just a shift in how candidates raise money, argues Michael Cornfield in the following viewpoint. The success of Internet support efforts demonstrates that ordinary citizens can participate in the political process alongside special interests. Internet networks not only raised money, but also increased citizen participation in other aspects of presidential campaigns, Cornfield claims. While the impact of grassroots Internet efforts on the broader political process remains unknown, it could be significant, he concludes. Cornfield, a political scientist and an advisor, is the author of Politics Moves Online: Campaigning and the Internet.

As you read, consider the following questions:

1. What does Michael Cornfield assert is now beyond dispute?

Michael Cornfield, "New Media, New Voters: Online Small Donors and the Future of Democratic Politics," The Century Foundation, Inc., February 21, 2008. Reproduced by permission.

2. What examples of a sense of voter commitment beyond campaign contributions does the author see?
3. What are some of the questions about small donors the author raises?

The financial disclosure reports of the presidential candidates for the year 2007 and January 2008 contain important news for the professional political community: Online small donors have arrived in force. After a decade of brilliant flashes, including, most recently, the "money bomb," millions sent to Ron Paul, Internet fund-raising has been turned into a steady flame. In 2008, Barack Obama's campaign received more than one million dollars every day, from a network of givers about to welcome its one millionth member.

It is now beyond dispute that a properly constructed campaign can draw upon the contributions of a great many people in sufficient amounts over a lengthy period of time. It can make itself financially competitive with campaigns relying on the traditional methods of high-roller finance committees, exclusive events, and PAC [political action committee] contributions. The money acquired online still heads mostly to traditional media, especially television. This points to the political Achilles' heel of the Internet: A campaign cannot use this new medium effectively to reach people who have not already indicated an interest in its candidate.

Shocking the Status Quo

But Obama's millions nevertheless reflect something new in how election campaigns operate, and potentially something new for policy making as well. Here's a cutaway view of how the process works. Last Sunday (February 17, [2008]) a lawyer I know sent an e-mail to seventeen of her friends, asking them to click to her personal fund-raising page and help her reach her goal of collecting $1,000 for Obama that week. The page was constructed for her use by the campaign. Those who responded favorably were asked on the screen they saw after completing the transaction to send a similar appeal to ten friends. A thank you e-mail from the Obama campaign arrived the next day, with links and invitations to Web pages organizing other kinds of volunteer activity. The day after that, a second e-mail from the campaign landed in the donors' inbox. The text of this "Major News" missive heralded the approach of the one millionth contributor thusly:

"This unprecedented foundation of support has built a campaign that has shaken the status quo and proven that ordinary people can compete in a political process too often dominated by special interests."

"Unlike Senator [Hillary] Clinton or Senator [John] McCain, we haven't taken a dime from Washington lobbyists or special interest PACs. Our campaign is responsible to no one but the people."

The request for another donation, with a deadline of March 4 [2008] (the day before the Ohio and Texas primaries) was followed with this link: "donate.barackobama.com/promise."

The benefits that small donor networks confer on campaigns are quite clear: much lower costs per acquisition, quicksilver cycles of solicitation and contribution, a back-end database with dossiers on the preferences and predilections of donors—in sum: a digital machine capable of generating a valuable revenue stream for the length of a campaign. A $100 donor can donate 22 times before an election, so smart campaigners craft serialized communications, referencing the media narrative so as to elicit money to make the next turning point go the way the donor and the campaigner both want to see happen. For instance, no sooner had word broken of Hillary Clinton's $5 million loan to her campaign than the Obama campaign announced a small donor drive to match it. Shameless, yes, but it engages citizens. Cues to small donors to give again come also from neighbors, the news itself, and, in the

Internet Donors Feel a Sense of Empowerment

This year's [2008's] passion for politics has fused with the ease of spending money on the Internet to create a new breed of supergivers of relatively small amounts. [Many such] donors say their frequent giving empowers their sense of involvement. . . .

"I think every election, they say this is the year online donations and the Internet are going to have an impact," said Johns Hopkins University political researcher Alexis Rice. "But this year, it's really the case."

Internet donations now dominate presidential politics. . . .

But it's not just the ease of donating that has made the Internet such a powerful campaign tool, Rice said. It's the ability of supporters to set their own campaign agendas online.

"Overall, the biggest difference between this election and previous ones is really the power given to the supporters," Rice said. "The supporters are going online and doing their own activism."

Burt Hubbard,
"Serial Donors: Supergivers Find Niche on the Net,"
Rocky Mountain News, *April 13, 2008.*

case of Obama (and others who campaign against "special interests," which is seemingly everyone), a meta-motivation of changing the way politics works.

Soliciting Commitment

What is being solicited, and acquired, along with the money, is a sense of voter commitment to campaign "contributions" in the general sense of the word, that is, to other modes of political participation, in addition to monetary contributions. One could see in the short term, for example, the Obama campaign (and, for that matter, the Clinton campaign, too) asking its super-donors (the ones who have not only given money, but set up pages to raise money) to rally their micro-networks and contact superdelegates within their collective orbits. Another call to action could enlist e-mailers to bat down a biased news story or online rumor. Not every "ask" has to be just for money. And when answers show results, as well as attentiveness, the money comes in without directly asking.

What this means for government and democracy won't become clear until after the election [in November 2008]. And that will depend on the beneficiary's willingness to make good on the message of change. Will the legions of small donors (one can hardly imagine how many entries will be in the victor's database) be summoned to send e-mails to Congress and the media on behalf of the election mandate? Will the small donors be melded with other campaign networks (centered around YouTube channels and Facebook groups, for instance) to form a multi-cause grassroots lobby? An ad hoc grassroots lobby stopped bipartisan, corporate-backed immigration reform twice in two years (with the considerable assistance of talk radio). What could an organized counterpart with the seal of the president as its icon accomplish in, say, the first one hundred days of the new administration?

There's your ultimate audacity.

Periodical Bibliography

The following articles have been selected to supplement the diverse views presented in this chapter.

Nancy Benac — "The People in Obama's Army of Small Donors," Associated Press, May 8, 2008.

Seth Finkelstein — "Great Internet Campaigns Don't Guarantee Success in Politics," *Guardian* (UK), February 14, 2008.

Scott Helman — "Small Donors Play Huge Role," *The Boston Globe*, April 10, 2008.

Terry Jones — "Internet Is Key to Political Campaigns: For Those Younger than 50, Half Are Checking Out Political News on the Internet," *St. Louis Journalism Review*, July/August, 2008.

Andrew Malcolm — "Top of the Ticket; Obama's Small-Donor 'Myth,'" *Los Angeles Times*, November 30, 2008.

Greg Mitchell — "The 2008 Campaign: The 'Last Hurrah'?" *Editor & Publisher*, December 2008.

Barack Obama — "The System Is Broken," *USA Today*, June 20, 2008.

Fredreka Schouten — "Small Doors Can Be Big Deal for Candidates," *USA Today*, October 19, 2007.

Lee Thornton — "New Media and the Man," *American Journalism Review*, December 2008.

Lynne Tillman — "The Virtual President," *Artforum*, January 2009.

Jose Antonio Vargas — "TechPresident, the Internet Citizenry's Consensus Taker," *The Washington Post*, October 3, 2007.

Linton Weeks — "Did Obama Kill Public Campaign Finance," NPR, April 20, 2009.

For Further Discussion

Chapter 1

1. Thomas E. Mann and Norman J. Ornstein contend that campaign finance reform laws have effectively reduced influence peddling and made political campaigns more competitive. Bradley A. Smith disagrees. He argues that such laws make campaigns less competitive because they stifle political speech. How do the rhetorical strategies of the authors differ? Which strategy do you find more persuasive?
2. David Corn and Byron York agree that issue ads sponsored by special interest groups can have a significant impact on political campaigns. They differ, however, on how to mediate their influence. What evidence does each author use to support his method of addressing concerns about issue ads? Which type of evidence do you find more persuasive?
3. Ilya Shapiro asserts that caps on campaign contributions protect incumbents. Deborah Goldberg cites studies that claim the opposite is true. How does each author address the claims of the opposing view? Is one method more persuasive than the other?
4. John Samples believes that public financing has failed. Farhad Manjoo suggests a unique, untested public financing solution to campaign finance corruption. Do you think Manjoo's strategy would overcome any of Samples's concerns?
5. What do the viewpoints on both sides of the debates in this chapter have in common and how do they differ? Explain your answers, citing from the viewpoints.

Chapter 2

1. Ed Kilgore claims public funding will promote fair congressional campaigns. Nathan Benefield disagrees. How does the audience for each author's viewpoint differ? Do you think the authors' rhetoric changes as a result? Based on these considerations, which do you find more persuasive?
2. Darrell M. West and John G. Geer differ in their views on the impact of attack ads in political campaigns. What examples do the authors cite to support their points of view? Which examples do you find persuasive?
3. Sarah O'Leary believes that federal agencies should protect voters from media manipulation. Brian Darling sees media regulation as a way to limit public access to ideas. What role does each author believe the media should play in political campaigns? How does this perspective influence his or her persuasiveness?
4. Identify where, if at all, West, Geer, O'Leary, and/or Darling explain what role the voting public should play in interpreting political campaign messages disseminated by the media. What do you think is the voting public's responsibility when listening to radio, watching television, or using the Internet?
5. What commonalities among the evidence and rhetoric can you find in the viewpoints on both sides of the debate in this chapter? What impact do these strategies have on the viewpoints' persuasiveness? Explain, citing from the viewpoints.

Chapter 3

1. Thomas E. Mann claims that reform will reduce partisan redistricting plans. Dan Seligson argues that redistricting reform is unlikely because political parties will support any plans that give their party the advantage. Do you

think any of Mann's reform strategies address Seligson's concerns? Explain why or why not.

2. Scott M. Lesowitz and Steven Hill disagree about the effectiveness of independent commissions and their ability to reduce partisan redistricting. Hill claims that in states with independent commissions, elections have not been any more competitive. Do you think this evidence is adequate to determine whether these commissions are effective? What other factors explored in this book might explain why elections have not been competitive? Do you think any of Lesowitz's suggestions to improve the process will overcome Hill's objections?
3. Tracie Powell asserts that redistricting plans sometimes hurt minority voters because these plans make it more difficult for minorities to elect people who represent their interests. She suggests strengthening the Voting Rights Act, civil rights legislation that was developed to prevent racist election practices. Some argue that redistricting plans, even if politically motivated, are not racially motivated. Do you agree? What evidence can you find in Powell's viewpoint that redistricting plans are racially motivated? What evidence, if any, found in the other viewpoints in this chapter suggests that they may not be racially motivated. How does this evidence impact your opinion?
4. Stuart Taylor maintains that U.S. Supreme Court rulings on redistricting are so confused that the Court appears unlikely to address the issue. Who do you think should address problems of partisan redistricting? The courts? The U.S. Congress? The states? Explain, citing the viewpoints in this chapter.

Chapter 4

1. Janette Kenner Muir maintains that the Internet has increased citizen engagement in and added transparency to political campaigns. Julian Sanchez warns that the Internet

may make it easier to spread misinformation or to engage in voter suppression. Do you think the Internet's advantages outweigh its disadvantages? Should something be done to protect Internet users? Do the viewpoints of West, Geer, O'Leary, and/or Darling in Chapter 2 impact your answer?

2. Kevin Diaz and Jay Mandle disagree over the impact of small donors on campaign finance. What evidence does each author cite to support his claim? Which do you find more persuasive?
3. Identify the different rhetorical strategies used by the authors in this chapter who explore the impact of small donors. Which strategy do you think is most persuasive? Explain your answer, citing from the viewpoints.
4. All of the viewpoints in this chapter were written during the 2008 election year. How do you think the ongoing political campaigns impacted the viewpoints? Do you think any of the authors would change their points of view based on the outcome of the election?

Organizations to Contact

The editors have compiled the following list of organizations concerned with the issues debated in this book. The descriptions are derived from materials provided by the organizations. All have publications or information available for interested readers. The list was compiled on the date of publication of the present volume; the information provided here may change. Be aware that many organizations take several weeks or longer to respond to inquiries, so allow as much time as possible.

Accuracy in Media (AIM)
4455 Connecticut Avenue NW, Suite 330
Washington, DC 20008
(202) 364-4401 • fax: (202) 364-4098
e-mail: info@aim.org
Web site: www.aim.org

Accuracy in Media (AIM) is a conservative watchdog organization. It researches claims of errors of fact made by the liberal news media and requests that the errors be corrected publicly. AIM publishes the bimonthly *AIM Report*, a weekly syndicated newspaper column, and the periodic *Media Monitor*. Commentary on campaign finance, redistricting, small campaign donors, and the influence of the Internet is available on its Web site.

Brennan Center for Justice at NYU School of Law
161 Avenue of the Americas, 12th Floor
New York, NY 10013
(212) 998-6730 • fax: (212) 995-4550
e-mail: brennancenter@nyu.edu
Web site: www.brennancenter.org

The Brennan Center for Justice at New York University School of Law is a research, education, and advocacy organization that focuses on concerns related to democracy and justice. In

June 2009 the center hosted the conference "Money in Politics 2009: New Horizons for Reform," publications from which are available on its Web site. The center's Web site also publishes articles, reports, and commentary, including *Electoral Competition and Low Contribution Limits* and *Breaking Free with Fair Elections*.

Campaign Finance Institute (CFI)
George Washington University, 1990 M Street NW, Suite 380
Washington, DC 20036
(202) 969-8890 • fax: (202) 969-5612
e-mail: info@cfinst.org
Web site: www.cfinst.org.

Campaign Finance Institute (CFI) is a nonprofit and nonpartisan research organization that studies issues related to campaign finance and develops reports and recommendations for government officials and the general public. CFI tracks political party fund-raising and contributions, and spending by congressional and presidential candidates. Many of CFI's publications are available on its Web site.

The Campaign Legal Center (CLC)
1640 Rhode Island Avenue NW, Suite 650
Washington, DC 20036
(202) 736-2200 • fax: (202) 736-2222
e-mail: info@campaignlegalcenter.org
Web site: www.campaignlegalcenter.org.

The Campaign Legal Center (CLC) is a research and public advocacy organization that examines the legal issues surrounding campaign finances and election law. The center tracks legal cases and issues reports and comments to the Federal Election Commission (FEC). Its Media Policy Program lobbies on behalf of open broadcast airwaves and participates in public forums on campaign media legislation. On its Web site, CLC publishes fact sheets, weekly reports, and articles of interest on current cases, Federal Election Commission proceedings, campaign finance reform, and redistricting.

Center for Competitive Politics (CCP)
901 North Glebe Road, Suite 900, Arlington, VA 22203
(703) 682-9359 • fax: (703) 682-9321
e-mail: info@campaignfreedom.org
Web site: www.campaignfreedom.org.

Center for Competitive Politics (CCP) was founded in 2005 by former Federal Election Commission chairman Bradley A. Smith. It promotes a more fair and open electoral process. The center publishes legal briefs, reports, and studies on campaign finance, which are available on its Web site. Center members often testify before Congress and other public bodies, and testimony transcripts are also available on its Web site.

Center for Information Technology and Society (CITS)
2215 North Hall, University of California
Santa Barbara, CA 93106
Web site: www.cits.ucsb.edu

Center for Information Technology and Society (CITS) is a multidisciplinary research center that studies the social effects of information technology. Faculty associated with the center represent diverse disciplinary perspectives, including art, English, sociology, communications, computer science, and electrical engineering. Its Web site provides access to articles, blogs, and videos of center events, including the article "Pursuing Social Change Online: The Use of Four Protest Tactics on the Internet"; blog posts from center members such as "Studying the Relationship Between the Internet, New Media and Politics" and "Campaigns and Technology"; and a video lecture by political science professor Bruce Bimber.

Center for Responsive Politics (CRP)
1101 Fourteenth Street NW, Suite 1030
Washington, DC 20005-5635
(202) 857-0044 • fax: (202) 857-7809
e-mail: info@crp.org
Web site: www.opensecrets.org

Center for Responsive Politics (CRP) tracks money in politics and its effect on public policy. Its Web site provides detailed information on funding sources for presidential and congressional incumbents, challengers, political action committees (PACs), and 527 committees. The center publishes the newsletter *Capital Eye* and numerous reports, including *The Millionaire on the Ballot* and *Shopping in (Partisan) Style*, which are available on its Web site.

Common Cause
1133 Nineteenth Street NW, 9th Floor
Washington, DC 20036
(202) 833-1200
e-mail: grassroots@commoncause.org
Web site: www.commoncause.org.

Founded in 1970, Common Cause is a nonprofit, nonpartisan advocacy group. Its goal is to hold elected leaders accountable to the American people. Common Cause promotes a variety of activist causes such as campaign finance reform, voter registration drives, and openness in government. It has led voter mobilization drives prior to presidential elections and efforts to enact public financing of elections at the state level. Its Web site has an archive of its online journal, *Common Cause Magazine*, and links to other publications, including research papers, press releases, and blogs.

Democracy 21
1875 I Street NW, 9th Floor, Washington, DC 20006
(202) 429-2008
Web site: www.democracy21.org.

Founded in 1997 by former Common Cause president Fred Wertheimer, Democracy 21 works to eliminate the undue influence of big money in American politics and to ensure the integrity and fairness of government decisions and elections. The organization promotes campaign finance reform and other political reforms to accomplish these goals. On its Web site, Democracy 21 publishes issue papers on the Bipartisan

Campaign Reform Act (BCRA), public financing, the Federal Election Commission, and 527 committees. The organization also publishes summaries of related court cases, opinions, briefs, commentary, and reports such as "Mayday, Mayday at the Federal Election Commission" and "Presidential Public Financing: Repairing the System" on its Web site.

Democratic National Committee (DNC)
430 South Capitol Street SE, Washington, DC 20003
(202) 863-8000
Web site: www.democrats.org.

Democratic National Committee (DNC) is the governing body of the Democratic Party in the United States. The partisan organization provides information on major national and state issues. It also offers details on how to get involved in political campaigns and provides information on Democratic candidates and campaign events. The DNC Web site examines contemporary legislation and legal issues from a Democratic perspective, and provides details about the party organization and structure.

Federal Election Commission (FEC)
999 E Street NW, Washington, DC 20463
(800) 424-9530
Web site: www.fec.gov

In 1975 Congress created the Federal Election Commission (FEC) as an independent regulatory agency. Its role is to administer and enforce the Federal Election Campaign Act (FECA), the statute that governs the financing of federal elections. The FEC discloses campaign finance information, enforces the provisions of the law such as the limits and prohibitions on contributions, and oversees the public funding of presidential elections. The Web site provides useful information about campaign finance issues and the laws and regulations governing this matter.

Institute for Politics, Democracy & the Internet (IPDI)
The Graduate School of Political Management
The George Washington University, Washington, DC 20052
(202) 994-1003 • fax: (202) 994-3346
e-mail: ipdi@ipdi.org
Web site: www.ipdi.org

Institute for Politics, Democracy & the Internet (IPDI) is a research institute at George Washington University that studies online politics. Its mission is to promote the use of the Internet and new communications technology in politics to enhance democratic values, encourage citizen participation, and improve governance. The institute conducts research that anticipates and interprets trends. It publishes a semi-annual online journal of research, commentary, and analysis on technology and politics, studies, guides, and articles, which are available on its Web site, including "Small Donors and Online Giving" and "The Audience for Political Blogs: New Research on Blog Readership."

Media Matters for America
625 Massachusetts Avenue NW, Suite 300
Washington, DC 20036
(202) 756-4100
Web site: http://mediamatters.org

Media Matters for America is an online progressive research and information center that monitors, analyzes, and corrects conservative misinformation in the U.S. media. On its Web site, Media Matters posts rapid-response analysis and publishes longer research and analytic reports that document conservative misinformation throughout the media. Media Matters also publishes articles on conservative misinformation during political campaigns.

Public Campaign
1320 Nineteenth Street NW, Suite M-1
Washington, DC 20036
(202) 293-0222 • fax: (202) 293-0202

e-mail: mengle@publicampaign.org
Web site: www.publiccampaign.org

Public Campaign is a nonpartisan campaign finance reform organization that seeks to reduce the role of special interest money in American politics. It publishes educational materials on various campaign reform measures and provides news, polling data, and commentary on money in politics on its Web site.

Republican National Committee (RNC)
310 First Street SE, Washington, DC 20003
(202) 863-8500
Web site: www.gop.com

Republican National Committee (RNC) is the governing body of the Republican Party, also known as the Grand Old Party (GOP). This partisan political group offers information on significant national and state issues, political involvement, and voter guides. RNC also provides information on Republican candidates, primaries, and campaign events. Its Web site analyzes issues from a Republican perspective and provides an overview of the party's organization and structure.

Bibliography of Books

William L. Benoit	*Communication in Political Campaigns*. New York: Peter Lang, 2007.
Steve Bickerstaff	*Lines in the Sand: Congressional Redistricting in Texas and the Influence of Tom DeLay*. Austin: University of Texas Press, 2007.
Bruce Bimber and Richard Davis	*Campaigning Online: The Internet in U.S. Elections*. New York: Oxford University Press, 2003.
Thomas L. Brunell	*Redistricting and Representation: Why Competitive Elections Are Bad for America*. New York: Routledge, 2008.
Bruce E. Cain, Todd Donovan, and Caroline J. Tolbert, eds.	*Democracy in the States: Experiments in Election Reform*. Washington, DC: Brookings Institution Press, 2008.
Dewey M. Clayton	*African Americans and the Politics of Congressional Redistricting*. New York: Routledge, 1999.
Michael Cornfield	*Politics Move Online: Campaigning and the Internet*. New York: Century Foundation Press, 2004.
Anthony Corrado, Thomas E. Mann, and Trevor Potter, eds.	*Inside the Campaign Finance Battle: Court Testimony on the New Reforms*. Washington, DC: Brookings Institution Press, 2003.

Anthony Corrado, et al.	*The New Campaign Finance Sourcebook*. Washington, DC: Brookings Institution Press, 2005.
Victoria A. Farrar-Myers and Diana Dwyre	*Limits & Loopholes: The Quest for Money, Free Speech, and Fair Elections*. Washington, DC: CQ Press, 2008.
David M. Farrell and Rüdiger Schmitt-Beck, eds.	*Do Political Campaigns Matter? Campaign Effects in Elections and Referendums*. New York: Routledge, 2002.
Peter F. Galderisi	*Redistricting in the New Millennium*. Lanham, MD: Lexington Books, 2005.
Daniel A. Gross and Robert K. Goidel	*The States of Campaign Finance Reform*. Columbus: Ohio State University Press, 2003.
Lisa Handley and Bernard Grofman, eds.	*Redistricting in Comparative Perspective*. New York: Oxford University Press, 2008.
Paul S. Herrnson, ed.	*Guide to Political Campaigns in America*. Washington, DC: CQ Press, 2005.
Steven Hill	*Fixing Elections: The Failure of America's Winner Take All Politics*. New York: Routledge, 2002.
Gary C. Jacobson	*Politics of Congressional Elections*. Upper Saddle River, NJ: Longman, 2008.

Michael J. Malbin, ed. *The Election After Reform: Money, Politics, and the Bipartisan Campaign Reform Act*. Lanham, MD: Rowman & Littlefield, 2006.

Thomas E. Mann and Bruce E. Cain, eds. *Party Lines: Competition, Partisanship, and Congressional Redistricting*. Washington, DC: Brookings Institution Press, 2005.

Mark S. Monmonier *Bushmanders and Bullwinkles: How Politicians Manipulate Electronic Maps and Census Data to Win Elections*. Chicago: University of Chicago Press, 2001.

Michael Nelson *The Elections of 2008*. Washington, DC: CQ Press, 2009.

Greg Palast *The Best Democracy Money Can Buy*. New York: Plume, 2004.

Mark E. Rush and Richard L. Engstrom *Fair and Effective Representation? Debating Electoral Reform and Minority Rights*. Lanham, MD: Rowman & Littlefield, 2001.

John C. Samples *The Fallacy of Campaign Finance Reform*. Chicago: University of Chicago Press, 2006.

Frederic Charles Schaffer *The Hidden Costs of Clean Election Reform*. Ithaca, NY: Cornell University Press, 2008.

Richard J. Semiatin, ed. *Campaigns on the Cutting Edge*. Washington, DC: CQ Press, 2008.

Rodney A. Smith	*Money, Power, & Elections: How Campaign Finance Reform Subverts American Democracy*. Baton Rouge: Louisiana State University Press, 2006.
Joe Trippi	*The Revolution Will Not Be Televised: Democracy, the Internet and the Overthrow of Everything*. New York: Regan Books, 2004.
Stephen Wayne	*The Road to the White House 2008*. Florence, KY: Wadsworth, 2007.
Jonathan Winburn	*The Realities of Redistricting: Following the Rules and Limiting Gerrymandering in State Legislative Redistricting*. Lanham, MD: Lexington Books, 2008.
Tinsley E. Yarbrough	*Race and Redistricting: The Shaw-Cromartie Cases*. Lawrence: University Press of Kansas, 2002.

Index

C

F

G

H

J

K

L

M

T

U

V